SUPERLATIVE WOMEN

STORIES OF WOMEN, SHINING LIGHT IN DARK PLACES

VISIONARY AUTHORS

SIERRA CLARK & WANDA HAWKINS

Superlative Women

Stories Of Women Shinning Light In Dark Places

Discover their voices, find strength in the dark, and showing how to heal from the inside

Copyright Page

Copyright © 2022 by Sierra M. Clark and Wanda Hawkins (ISBN)

Paperback 979-8218-10543-3

E-Book 979-8-218-105455-0

Published by: Sierra M. Clark and Wanda Hawkins

Cover design: (Arif Hossain) Own your Story Team

Layout and type setting: Sierra M. Clark

Editor: Tyenisha Reed (I 'am Queen)

TABLE OF CONTENTS

STORIES OF WOMEN SHINING LIGHT IN DARK PLACES

DEDICATION

To women and girls globally, thank you for being a part of this fabric that makes us Superlative. To every famine energy, in the restraints and freedom of our flesh.

Please know who you are!

To be internally and wonderfully made, grow, and blossom like it. To apply knowledge equals wisdom.

Never deny the power you are; magic is just the icing.

To every famine energy that created a way out of no way. To all the radicalness you selfishly hold for yourself.

To be sure you have a life well lived. To be intentional with everything you birth.

This work will be a beaming light for the world to see.

To our duty and privilege to heal, and be recovered from the inside out.

FOREWORD

Those familiar with my message know that I love the concept of standing in your story and not in it. As a visionary author of my book, Embracing Imperfections, I love how this book was beautifully put together.

With the turn of EVERY page of this book, I found myself happy that I've learned how to embrace my imperfections. What this anthology shines a light on, I can say I've personally experienced or have seen the darkness in the women population. Sierra and Wanda have joined forces to ensure the everyday women they call shores don't become victims of their life's story.

They use this Anthology to allow these sheroes to discover their voices. Standing up to the things they've experienced in the dark, the things they've painfully smiled through and felt powerless to. This Anthology gives you action steps you can take to go from victim to victor.

This anthology does a beautiful job highlighting the power of collaboration, one can't do alone what we can do together. I've seen with my own eyes and experienced the physical and holistic benefits when women can use their weaknesses as strength and become stronger together—allowing their uniqueness to be reflections of one another, not a reason to envy or be jealous.

It doesn't surprise me that these two Superlative women have come together like Batman and Robin to fight against and with everyday sheroes. Both of them have slayed their share of villains and dragons. (read their Bio)

Sierra's chapter is titled Reflections Of Her, and Wanda's chapter is titled Finding My Superpower. This is how Superlative Woman was born, and it reveals oozes of gentle, strong reminders to women globally.

Superlative – means to the highest degree, to the highest form. And the things we experience cannot take that away. However, feelings and thoughts can help us feel otherwise about this fact.

An important message to women is that they individually have the superpower of being Superlative on a real-life budget. Another high importance that has been sent out like the Bat signal with each pace of this Anthology is it is time to reap the benefits and create the magic of being connected to another woman.

This Anthology has allowed sheroes from all walks of life to shine a light on tragic, heartbreaking, overwhelming moments in time. Showing you how they decided to no longer let their imperfections, wrong turns, and regrets, should and could have been their kryptonite. Women dispel darkness, stand up to their stories, and show how to heal from the inside out. Finally, join focuses like never before. Becoming a

beaming light to be seen all over the world. This is more than a book; it's history in the making.

"Being superlative isn't optional; it's natural"

-Sierra M. Clark

Superlative Women could be the sequel for Embracing Imperfection vol 1,2, and 3, which encourages women to stand on their story, not in it.

Jessica T. Moore

PREFACE

We are two women who feel that we were divinely connected to create safe spaces for women to learn holistic ways to heal from the inside out. The call was accepted, so they wrote the vision and made it plain.

There is no other way of doing this than to take intentional looks inside the mirror, the only way out is in. Sierra and Wanda both agree that the most authentic form of doing so was through their willingness to see their reflection in other women.

So they invested in becoming Visionary Authors. This would not only create a safe space, but it will also permit us to awaken as sleeping beauties. We will be able to see the beauty and scars we collectively share as women.

To reignite the power that lives in each of us. That will grow in strength as we shine light in dark places and intentionally heal.

To become like a generator, a live wire to power centuries to come. This will provide light in all places. Allowing every woman to see that she's superlative, even in dark moments.

ACKNOWLEDGMENTS

To all the behind the scene people, to the fill-in-the-blank people, to the lover of our soul. To the Sheroes we titled Co-Authors, who thought it not robbery to be a foundational part of this Anthology. To every wrong turn that led us, right to where we needed to go.

DEANNA SMITH
Don't Count Me Out

Quote

"When you are making a pro and con list about me, make sure you remember I am making one as well!"

Biography

Deanna Smith is the founder of JW Lyles Legacy LLC, currently offering bookkeeping and business consulting. After years of self-doubt and challenges with understanding who God created her to be, her passion and commitment are to encourage others to succeed in their purpose and vision. Her love of God and past experiences of being underestimated drives her to be the best version of herself. It is her desire that her legacy is one of hope over despair, courage over fear, and love over hate.

Currently, a vision partner with Divine Destiny Center, where her focus is mentoring young girls to ensure they are better equipped for the challenges of the world, as well as volunteering with other outreaches working with women to help them recover and get back on the path of God's plan for them. In her business, she hopes to see visions from God implemented and successful for the kingdom. She is a daughter, mother, sister, accountant, entrepreneur, teacher, avid learner, and a born leader. Her experiences in these roles, though her own, can be used to help and assist others in making choices that will align with what they want to see and with what God is asking them to do.

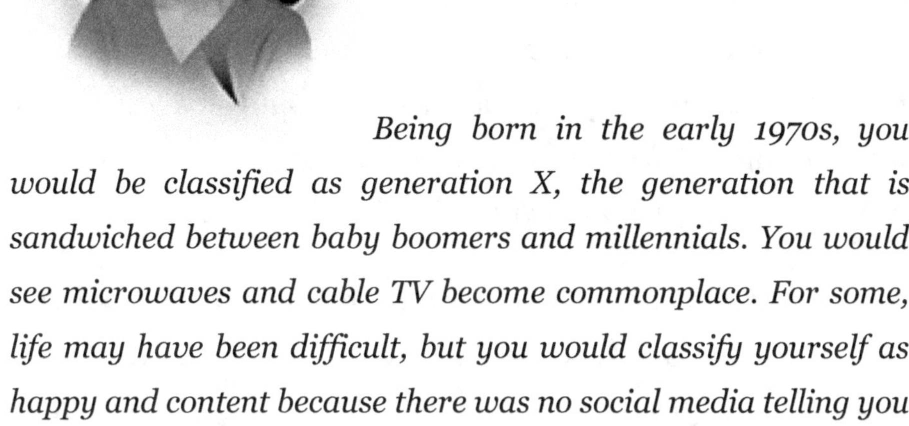

Being born in the early 1970s, you would be classified as generation X, the generation that is sandwiched between baby boomers and millennials. You would see microwaves and cable TV become commonplace. For some, life may have been difficult, but you would classify yourself as happy and content because there was no social media telling you differently. This story begins with two teens who became parents before many saw it as their time.

The dad was the high school jock who had every girl in school wanting a chance to be on his arm, while the mom was the quiet one that was "just his friend." She would spend her life being a combination of both; soft and a nerd but athletic and part of the "it" crowd so she struggled for years trying to find her place because she struggled to find where she belonged. Never seems to be the first choice in either scenario because for some reason or another. Her parents both turned 17 within months of the birth of their first child. The world was different then.

Mothers had to leave school to be taken to a school-specific for pregnant teens, where young moms were just spending the day in hiding. A pregnant teen girl was not something they wanted other young girls to see. As a child, they would tell their daughter she could be and do anything she wanted to do. Therefore, the daughter determined she would be the best at everything; piano playing, grades on her report card, softball, basketball, etc.. In everything she would participate in, she would give her all. She would compete with whomever she deemed was better than her, even if there was no competition.

She wanted everyone to look at her, the daughter of teen parents, as someone who could do it all and do it all well. She didn't want to be excluded from any conversation. She wanted someone to pick her first! Early on, she wanted to be a teacher like her kindergarten teacher, the first person she ever interacted with who didn't look like anyone in her community. She wanted to inspire and teach little kids to be great. Since her parents were both teens, she ultimately would grow up with her mother and grandmother, who would steer her toward her studies. Getting good grades and reading in her spare time would be her getaway and ultimately help her reach her greater goals. There were few words of affirmation in her home as this was not the family's way, but she was well taken care of.

Teachers would praise her for being top of the class and an overachiever of sorts. She spent her time doing all she could to get the acknowledgement of doing a good job. When she shared her goal of being a teacher with family members, she was told she was too smart for that. So, she needed to aim higher. Growing up in a small town that still has visible signs of segregation made it difficult to see past her immediate surroundings, so she needed to determine what that thing would be. The statistics for a child born to teen parents then were not in her favor. She needed something that would allow her to help others see beyond their surroundings.

Then there were comments about not expecting too much or not setting herself up for failure because life is not fair. As she started to gain siblings, she didn't want that to be what her siblings were hearing, or any other kids for that matter. So, she did her best to prove them all wrong. She pressed on. As soon as she was of age and able, she got a job to pay her own way and provide additional training and classes needed to fulfill her dreams. At her high school graduation, after being in the top 10 of her class, donning honor society cords and all the other accolades, she went to her family for the celebration, and her mother, now with an additional three other children, looked her in her eyes and spoke.

"Wow, I didn't even know a GPA greater than 4.0 was possible. I just wanted you to graduate on time!" At that moment, she felt like all that hard work and dedication was for nothing. She debated internally why she stressed herself for all those years when she only needed to graduate on time, and no one would have expected anything more! Was her mom rejecting her hard work as so many others had? Was her mom like others rejecting her? As she grew older and matured, she knew her mom meant no harm, but her mom, being limited by her experiences, had already determined the category she wanted her daughter in.

Being a high school graduate who wasn't held back and had no kids was enough. Knowing she had nothing to prove to her mom, the daughter decided to go to school out of state, majoring in engineering because that aligned more with what she saw that others saw in her. Being away from home and being exposed to different people and different experiences was just what she needed to realize what had happened. In college, students meet many different people, but when a minority attends a predominantly white university, you meet yourself.

To explain, colleges and universities have a type, so when the applications come in, they look for those types that will "fit" their environment. Therefore, you meet many other students with many of the same boxes checked off, i.e., played sports, played an instrument, was on student council, etc. During the years of college life, she began to see how life up until that point felt like she was never enough. Through others, as they shared how they worked hard in their hometowns to prove others wrong about them, she realized it was easy for others to count someone not like them out. As she struggled through classes in what she thought she wanted to do with her life, she found peace in her elective classes that centered around religion and black studies.

In her dorm room, her roommate began to share her love of Christ and invited her to church. In those interactions, she learned more intimately about how God wants a relationship with the person, and He has a plan/purpose for each person from the very beginning. She also saw how even though perfect, people rejected Jesus himself! This was the beginning of the turning point.

Many years later, before her father died, he shared the story of how he denied being the father of that unborn baby and how his mom told him to never deny her ever again and he didn't. It took some time before she could understand why he would share such a story, but she realized that was her first rejection. This has been key to her maturing and walking with God. She had to overcome rejection because it made her put up walls preventing her from moving into positions needed for God's ultimate goal. The lesson learned was that people will put you in categories of their determination before they really get to know you. When you are born under particular circumstances or make choices that put you in those circumstances, God has a purpose for everything you experience. She didn't ask to be born to teen parents or be raised in a racially segregated town, but God knew that these things would be part of her story and how they were needed to push her to the right places.

Rejection is part of life and goes back to the book of Genesis. When God asked Adam why he ate the forbidden fruit, he answered, "It was the woman you gave me who gave me the fruit, and I ate it." (Genesis 3:12 ERV). Adam, in the prior chapter, was excited to have this woman, but how quickly he rejected her and told God, he was the one who brought her to him. What he didn't know was that God knew what would happen, and He would use it for the good of all.

Today through everything, that daughter of two seventeen-year-olds is a successful businesswoman who spends her free time teaching and encouraging girls and young women to be exactly who they are. Not allowing the world to define what God has already created and placing a demand for a particular end. Our lives have a plan and purpose, and the enemy or people (haters) don't want it to be fulfilled. At times, even those you love unknowingly are helping to discourage you, but you can't give up.

No matter what comes your way or what people may say if you don't quit, God will provide a way to overcome. Now, if you are in a dangerous relationship, you have to make moves to remove yourself.

God doesn't put us in relationships where we have not loved the way he has called us to be loved. Ask Him what needs to be done, and He will tell you when to make your moves safely and securely. If things are just difficult i.e., it's just hard, you must remember that God makes no mistakes. He knew exactly where you would be at this time, so you must keep pressing. Don't let anyone, even yourself count you out!

Michael Jordan is one of the greatest to ever play the game of basketball. He lost almost 300 games and missed over 9000 shots in his career, but no one ever counted him out if he had the ball in his hands with only seconds on the clock. He was still a threat to them. They would still guard him with a mission to stop him from scoring or changing what seemed like their time to win.

We have to apply that same tenacity to our everyday life. Even when it looks like we are losing, we win with God on our side. You can't be a threat to those things that will come against you if you quit! Be willing to stay in the game because God is working something out. If He is telling you to do or say something, it is not to put you in a losing situation. He created you, and he knows exactly why. Ask Him what it is you need to do, and let Him guide you. It won't always be easy, but there is peace when God is in control. Even

When the daughter of teen parents had no idea who God was, He was working things out. He knew what she would need to be encouraged, He knew what she would need to encourage others. Those moments of disappointment were so she would know what to say to others. Those moments of despair were so she could sympathize and have empathy for others as she listens.

The enemy and haters are still at work, not wanting us to complete the plan for our lives. If you want or have always wanted to have a degree, you should do it! If you want to start a business, do it! Your age, economic position, or anything else doesn't matter. If God needs you in that school or business for whatever is needed, He will provide everything that is needed to get you there and get you through it. When it is part of His plan, you will see doors opening that you never imagined. We have to stay in the game; don't quit and don't give up. Trusting God and who we are is key to our success.

Action Steps

First, write the vision and make it plain (Habakkuk 2:2). Many will encourage journaling, where you set time every day to write down what has happened or what you want to happen. Writing the vision is taking time to record those things that you consider to be a goal, whether God-given or not. When things get difficult, this becomes something that can be looked at to remind you why you are doing what you are doing. A reference point also gives you a view of how far you have come.

Second, do your research. This can be as simple as a Google search to ensure you have the right insight. This will allow you to make sure you have everything that is needed. To be an accountant, you actually don't have to have a degree in accounting. Just like when you are looking for directions on a map, many roads lead you to your destination. You just want to be on the road that God designed specifically for you. Making a pro and con list is helpful as it lists out why things would be good or why things would be bad; then you know what's the worst that can happen. The last research would be self-reflection as to your why. The daughter was trying to satisfy everyone but herself. Never knowing their expectations but striving to fulfill them. Don't discount or count out your own reasons for doing or being. Your why is more important than the rest.

Lastly, don't quit! A basketball game is not won with the whole team sitting on the sideline. The fans in the arena may or may not be cheering the team on, but they are not playing the game. You have to be in the game, and in the end, if God calls you to it, He will get you through it. He is the fan you want! He sent Jesus to ensure you had exactly what was needed to be the winner, no matter what it looked like. People may see you as less than but God sees you as more than a conqueror, so go and win!

Resources

Instagram @jwlyles_legacy

Facebook JWLyles Legacy LLC

ASHLEY DILLARD
You Are Not Your Experiences

Quote:

"You are whole, healed, and not the experiences of your journey." I Am That I Am Exodus 3:14

Biography

Ashley Dillard is an enthusiastic, straightforward woman who shares her life lessons with all willing and ready to elevate their lives. She was born in Dayton, OH. three months premature, prepared to enter this dimension in full force. She experienced life in many facets. In her journey, she has lived a life full of adventure, love, chaos, lessons, addiction, success, and perseverance.

Destined for greatness, she vowed to follow her heart and intuitive spirit, never letting situational circumstances dictate her destiny or destination. Turning adversity into opportunity and abandoning the victimhood mentality acquired through years of traumatic experiences, betrayal, neglect, abuse, learned behavior, and codependency.

Ashley is a wife, mother, author, and business owner and advocates for spiritual awakening, elevation, and operating these human experiences as the true expression of love we all are.

Her mission is to never forget who she is and her divine purpose, simultaneously being an example to others to live in their power and love with no conditions.

In December of 1983, I made my entrance to this dimension. The 22nd at 12:10 pm, to be exact. Three months earlier than the Doctors and my parents anticipated. Weighing 1 lb. 12 oz, births of this caliber were seen as risky and life-threatening at this time, with questionable survival and expected congenital disabilities. Many babies born three months premature have lifelong complications, breathing issues, underdeveloped brains and lungs, learning disabilities, and much more. I was able to escape lifelong complications.

I underwent surgery shortly after birth because my lungs were not fully developed, and I stayed in the hospital for almost 100 days in an incubator until my weight was 5lbs. Other than that, I was fine. I was small but still a fighter, determined and persistent. I still have a bump on my forehead where the tube was placed. To give you an idea of how small I was, I could fit in the palm of your hand; I was compared to the size of a coke can. What an entrance, right? Growing up knowing how my life started, I always felt I was born for a special reason and God had big plans for me. He allowed me to live and defy the odds of medicine. Little did I know all that I would experience in this life and the testimony I would be able to share.

The bell rings, and kids scramble to pack their backpacks and head to the line of yellow school buses to be transported home. It was the last day of fourth grade, and everyone was excited about summer break. I stared out the window in excitement, as I often did, and daydreamed about my new summer experiences. From the time I was two years old, I visited my maternal aunt in the summertime, and this year would be no different. I was eager to visit a new place, meet new people and enjoy time away from home. My aunt had a great career, and she relocated often. This allowed me to visit many different states and a completely different lifestyle. In all my excitement, I left a precious notebook on my desk. From a young age, I wanted to share my story with the world. I knew the life experiences I'd had and situations witnessed should be shared and could serve others. That is what I believed. What other reason could all this be happening? My life was like movies I'd seen, and at a young age, writing became a passion and was identified as a talent in elementary school. By this time, I had experienced a lifetime's worth of life-shaping events. All I had to do was write and tell the story

In the notebook, I wrote mostly about my pain points and how hectic life was living with parents who suffered from addiction, and what it looked and felt like from my 10-year-old perspective. I wrote out scenes and scenarios as I remembered them occurring. Each time my mom relapsed, the hospital visits when my dad had a Sickle Cell crisis, growing up calling two men dad, not knowing which was my biological father.

Spending time with both families and feeling like I was living a double life. Moving between parents' homes, abandonment, molestation, dysfunctional relationships, lack of consistent stability and how it shaped my understanding of the world, self-identity, self-esteem, and love of self. I wrote about living in the "trap", and how I would not become a victim of that life. I vowed to be and do differently than my parents had. I remember after losing the notebook, I was very sad; it was a traumatic experience. It felt like I'd lost a part of me that I would never get back. What I didn't know then was that the life experiences and the words on the page were not mines, other people's actions were not mine, and my life at this point was not "my fault."

Life with my parents was not all bad; like to say they were two smart, savvy, loyal, and loving individuals with unhealed traumas, unresolved issues, and underdeveloped emotional intelligence. All of which leads them to make poor choices based on their situations and circumstances multiple times. That does not make them bad people, just people who made unbeneficial choices. In the midst of all the chaos, I learned a lot from them. Commitment, dedication, hard work, unconditional love, loyalty, and perseverance.

By age 12, my two younger sisters were in foster care, and I was soon to be next. I remember the day social services visited my house and took my youngest sister away. Ironically, the caseworker knew who my mom was and notified me that my other sister (my mom's daughter) was also in foster care. Shortly after hearing this news, I made one of the most important phone calls of our lives. I called my aunt, who I visited every summer, and explained the situation. Not long after, about three months, my middle sister was living with her, and I decided to move in with her too. It was summertime, and California was the destination. I remember calling my dad over summer break and asking if I could stay, telling him I didn't want to return to Ohio. He said he would think about it, and the next day he called and told me I could stay. Later I would find out that he was going to prison, and my mom had relapsed, so I was in the best place.

The decision to move with my aunt was one of the most important things in my life. At such a young age, I had the ability to recognize a better situation and environment for myself and the courage to leave everything and everyone I'd known and choose what was best for me. I remember wanting to hurt my dad and not wanting to leave my sister. Ultimately, I chose myself, and I am grateful he allowed me to do so.

This would not be the last time I stood in my power, listened to my intuition, and followed my heart, but it was an amazing way to start and would prove beneficial.

Around the same time, I moved away from home; I stopped all communication with my "second dad's family. I recall thinking I could no longer live a lie. My whole life, all 12 years of it. I felt like I had betrayed who I knew as my biological dad by calling another man dad and spending time with the other family. My soul was tired, and it was emotionally draining. Looking back as an adult, I laugh because all the adults allowed this to happen. My mom and dad's knew what was happening, and their families played along. I would get picked up from one dad's house to go to the others.

Spending Holidays and vacations throughout the years. This experience taught me so much. Most importantly, I learned that things are not always what they seem, and your memories and beliefs can and will hold you back if not faced head-on.

It wasn't until recently that I discovered my dad's never met. They both loved my mom and loved me, so they decided that they would provide and give me the "best life" they could. I laugh now as I understand this as Ego in its best form. It would be nice to know the truth, but my dad never takes a test and has passed away, and I recently reconnected with my "second dad," who does not wish to take a test, even after over 20 years of no contact.

At this point, I feel blessed to have had two paternal families who loved me the best way they knew how and provided for me. Many people can't say they had one, let alone two dads. This experience taught me gratitude for sure.

One of the most challenging lessons I learned on this journey was to let go of being ashamed of where and who I came from. At times it felt like me telling my life experiences somehow would negatively affect me or alter the view others had of me. I remember not wanting to tell people why I lived with my aunt or where my parents were. I thought it would decrease my worth and value to others. I literally was measuring my self-worth based on the actions of my parents. I also did not want to diminish their character. Again, my parents were great people who made some bad choices, and like many other families, I was taught what happens at home stays at home.

My life in no way was "normal" by society's standards. I felt ashamed and embarrassed; after moving, it felt like I was the only one who had this story. I'd moved to southern California, where dreams come true. In my mind, I wanted to start over and create a "new life," a suburban life. I realized ignoring my past would not create my future; facing my past, and the feelings I had, talking to my parents, obtaining more details, and learning their inner struggles helped to gain an understanding of the events and know I had no responsibility for anything that transpired. This experience helped me to realize that our beliefs and memories aren't always facts and the illusions we create can be detrimental if not corrected.

Fortunately, I could rectify the stories I'd told myself, change my reflection, and move forward. I'm sharing this story because I know others have experienced similar situations and may feel like their childhood makes them uniquely defective. You may feel like you did something wrong or wonder why your life started out the way it did. I used to; I carried the labels created by society. I believed I was a survivor, which made me a victim. I listed many of them at the beginning of this chapter. The truth is none of that really matters. Life happened for me, not to me. I am not broken; I do not need to be fixed. I do not need to relive my life experiences to validate my actions. I am healed and whole. You are healed and whole.

No matter what the situation, you can choose right now to live in your power, not in your past. Living in the power of now does not mean you forget the lessons learned; it means you don't have to learn them again, and no cycle(s) to be broken. You can make the same stance today, right now. Do what is best for you. Love yourself unconditionally, listen to your inner voice and answer the call of your destiny. You deserve it.

If you are anything like me and sometimes just need to know what to do, you read the chapter and ask now, how do I apply any of this? What does stand in my power look like? I have included 3 Steps of Action below. When applied practical steps have been proven to lead to clarity, knowledge of self, and alignment with your divine purpose.

You must choose to choose yourself, daily, and make no excuses for showing up. Knowing you are divinely created for a purpose and never stop learning, growing, and moving forward. Speak life over yourself and visualize the experiences you desire. Remember life is happening for you, not happening to you. You deserve the best you.

Action Steps

Step One: Know Thyself.

Disclaimer- this does not happen overnight. It will take consistency and commitment.

With all your heart, you must know without a shadow of a doubt that you are divinely created, healed, and whole and that no mistake was made when you were created, and no one can be you but you. Be you unapologetically. Take the time to learn yourself again, that childhood knowledge. Sit still, meditate, listen to your inner voice, speak positively to yourself, do what feels good, remember what inspired you or what you naturally gravitated towards as a child, read, journal, spend time in nature, listen to meditation music, and healing frequencies, like 111hz, 222 hz, 963hz, speak words of affirmation.

Affirmations:

"I am divinely created"

"I am healed"

"I am whole"

Step Two: Never give up.

Many people quit on themselves when things don't go the way they planned or when they cannot see a way out or around what's in front of them. One thing I've learned is that life takes persistence and commitment. If one way doesn't yield the results desired, try another way. It is ok to change directions; just never stop moving forward. Continue to put one foot in front of the other every day. Be open to wise. counsel and never stop learning. Study and put in the hours required to master yourself. No does not mean never.

When things get tough, I say the following:

"Everything is working out for my good,"

"Everything is right on track,"

"I am right where I belong"

Step Three: Stop searching outside of yourself.

The Universe is inside of you. The love you desire is inside of you. Stop looking for validation. Permit yourself to love yourself unconditionally. Push past your fears. Be Honest with yourself and others about what is best for you. It's ok to say no. It is ok to live a life different from what you expect. It's ok to color outside the lines. Live in your truth even when it's uncomfortable.

When I'm disconnected from the love I am, I say these affirmations:

"No one can love you as I can"

"Self-love is the best love"

"I am a vibration of love having a human experience"

"Everything you ever wanted is on the other side of fear"

****38****

Resources

Website: www.vibezbyshe.com

IG: @AshleyDillard_Mindset_Mentor

KIMBERLY A. JACKSON

Lemons Or Lemonade It's Our Choice

QUOTE

"Let life obstacles prepare you not paralyze you."

Biography

Kimberly Jackson was born in Stroudsburg, Pennsylvania. She is the daughter of Ms. Lola Mae Byrd & Robert Hicks. She is the mother of two adult children, Ciara and Marcus. She has worked in Healthcare Customer Service & Management for 30-plus years, and she loves helping and assisting others.

Kimberly is ordained to Minister the Gospel and is a Certified Purpose Life Strategist Coach, Inspirational Speaker, Entrepreneur, and Visionary. Kimberly is

very involved with her church and has always had an assignment, even at a young age, for mentorship and helping others. Kimberly found herself mentoring young ladies early in her walk, and she knew it wasn't just something she enjoyed, but she had a call on her life.

Kimberly's testimony and passion have driven her commitment to mentoring and coaching women over the last 20 years through various organizations and opportunities. Kimberly decided to take the life challenges that impacted her as early as 19

years old and allow them to remind her that "QUITTING WAS NOT An OPTION".

Through it all, she knew she had to keep striving for victory and be that light and example for others.

Through ministry, she would teach bible study in the women's prison, go to the strip clubs monthly to encourage the ladies, and show them the love of God, and teach self-esteem

classes in the battered shelter and sex-trafficking safe houses, but even with that, she knew it was time to give birth to the assignment. A place of Restoration & Transformation.

Kimberly is the Founder and Executive Director of Divine Destiny Center Inc.,

I grew up as the youngest and only girl in a single-parent household; with three older brothers than me. We moved here from Pennsylvania when I was 5 or 6 years of age, and my mother was

the only provider in the home. I watched her day in and day out, going to work early and getting home early enough to ensure my brothers and I were taken care of. She was very protective of us and wanted us to have the best and not become a part of society's take on the children in our neighborhood. We didn't have everything, but we still lived a pretty good life.

My mother took a lot of time to share what it means to present yourself respectfully and always demand respect, and others will respect you. She also showed me that QUITTING was not an option or an excuse. Many of the children in my neighborhood would love to be at our house because they knew Ms. Lola was going to be there and was always available to talk and inspire them to be better. I guess you can say our house became a safe haven for many children, and I didn't mind sharing her because I figured, "I'll have her for a lifetime"

Life has a funny way of teaching your things even when you are not quite prepared. During my high school years, things started looking up for my mom, my brothers, and I, and we eventually moved to a rather nicer place. My mother was able to purchase a car she gave me during the 11th grade for me to attend the high school of my choice because there was no school bus in our new neighborhood. I was so excited; I graduated, and things were great, and soon after, I attended a local college majoring in computer information science. Things were going great; my grades were good, A's and B's, and I could get a part-time job as an executive secretary for American Express. Not so bad for an 18-year-old.

Life was good, and like many of us, I was just living life as if everything was going to remain, not knowing that not within a twelve-month span, my life would change forever, and it would take me for a loop. Life has a way of helping you grow up sooner than you expected. As I went about my life, I was sitting at my desk at work, and my mother called me and I could hear it in her voice that something was not quite right. She said, 'Kim, I just left the doctor's office, and they told me that I have to take some treatments to make my hair come out but not to worry". Me being 18 and knowing nothing about any medical stuff and, to be honest with you, never seen my mother a day in my life so I just brushed it off.

A few weeks went by, and I noticed a difference in my mother's behavior, and it began to bother me and my supervisor at the time asked me what was wrong. I explained to her what was going on, and low and behold, her husband was a physician, and she called him, and I told him about these treatments my mother was taking and how it made her feel. Again, I didn't know anything.

My supervisor, "her name was Anne " said to call your mother I wanted to tell her, and I did. Well, they spoke, and my mother told her what was going on and that she didn't feel I would be able to handle the news. My mother and I were close. After their conversation they set up a time for us all to meet along with a doctor and that is when I received the news and it hit me like a rock.

I could not believe my mother, who is only 49 years old" had cancer, and to make it even worth it was one that is very rare, and the survival percentage was very low. This changed my entire life in November 1989, and being told she only had six months took me on a downward spiral that I could see my way through. I didn't know God then, and confusion and fear overtook my life.

I instantly became a caregiver, cut my work hours, called my brothers, who lived out of state at that time, and informed them that we had to devise a plan. I tried to remain in school but had to cut my hours. In May 1990, my mother lost that battle to Cancer, and my life shifted in ways I never thought possible. I had my brothers, grandmother, and other family members, but it was a transition at 19 years of age and a young woman that I wouldn't want anyone to experience.

This was something at the time I really couldn't see my way through. It affected every area of my life: school, work, mental, and much more. I thank God for my grandmother. She did the best she could while she was mourning the loss of her daughter, the youngest of her two children. It was rough, and as I reflect on it now, I know God had me covered even during this time when I didn't know much about living a life for Christ, Faith. Prayer or any such thing.

I can honestly say I began a soul-searching journey, and during the next three years, I had to make some adjustments and seek peace because nothing I knew to do was working for me; I was struggling inside. Smiling on the outside; Drowning on the inside, you know how many of us do. We keep on moving, yet we are numb, but no one sees it. One day I knew I must do something, and I reached out for some assistance and counseling and was introduced to a wonderful Church that taught the word from there, my deliverance came, and I understood then that all this time, God was carrying me through.

This is just one of the trials that God has helped me overcome earlier in my walk, but I would tell anyone that there are times we feel all alone and lost. Busted and disgusted. Not knowing your next move, being blind-sided by the heaviness of what we maybe are experiencing to the point we can't see any light on the other side of the tunnel.

We have those thoughts in my mind like pops on Sanford and Son would say, "This is the big one.

" We found ourselves asking God ``Why Me? It's not fair. There will be moments we all face opportunity for fear, failure, disappointments, and devastating situations to enter our lives,

yet we must take control of every situation, and that process will start with a quote I heard a wise man once share "How we see the problem is the problem" which forces us to renew our minds.

The journey to healing and wholeness takes us doing our part. It's a process, and there is no quick fix or one-stop-shop in us reaching that feeling of wholeness. Healing is developing a sense of personal wholeness that involves physical, mental, emotional, social, and spiritual aspects of our human experience. We must take the time to be healed from our past hurts, anger, frustrations, and fears otherwise, we risk it defining our life. It is my prayer and desire that you begin this journey by reintroducing yourself to the new you.

Somewhere along the way, we find ourselves question to question that we were great and amazing- as we begin to believe again- list out the things that we know you are great at!!

There are keys to this journey- and here are a few things that I have figured out along the way. These keys can serve as a daily reminder to keep going!

Just for today, I open myself up to understand more

I upgrade my perspective- my perception of myself.

I trust myself with my power

I dare to explore more of myself and the world around me.

Action Steps

#1. Be intentional- Be intentional with your words, for it will lead to joy. The words say for us to be slow to speak. In this process, think before you speak, listen, and learn.

-Start your day with declarations and affirmations. Command your day with your words. For example,

Today I will be calm

Today I will be joyful

Today I will be grateful

Today I will acknowledge my uniqueness

Today I will be intentional about my journey

There is power in the words we speak. Though it's easy to simply express what we feel or to share what's on our minds, we need to make sure we are allowing our words to line up with what we want to receive. Be very intentional about what you declare in your day.

#2 Release

Release is where you forgive. Forgiveness starts within; therefore, you want to forgive yourself

I release my past mistakes and decisions

I release the fear of the unknown

I release the fear of being successful

I release all doubt & procrastination

Self-forgiveness helps us to resolve feelings of both guilt and shame. In this step, we not only release ourselves from self-served bondage, but this step opens the door for us to forgive others as well. The release of the hurt and pain helps us resolve feelings of guilt and shame by accepting responsibility for our actions, apologizing, and learning from our mistakes.

3# Believe

When we stop believing in ourselves, we become desperate and make different decisions. Self-efficacy builds our confidence, it allows us to achieve our goals. Believing in yourself allows you to manage and ensure direction. Daily declare your belief which will create strength; it ignites and activates our actions. For example,

I believe in myself

I believe that I have a right to be successful

I believe that I am equipped for greatness
I believe I deserve the best in life.

Resources

DivineDestinyCenter.com

KCM-LLC.org

@Facebook.com/midwife coaching

YOLANDA OWENS
Unshakable Faith

·49·

Quote

"Weeping May Endure for A Night but Joy Comes In the Morning."
Psalms 30:5

Biography

Yolanda Owen, a wife to Marion Owens. We have three adult children and five grandchildren. Yolanda a proud graduate of Roosevelt University with a Master of Science in Accounting, an entrepreneur, Tax specialist, and consultant. she has been a Christian most of my adult life. She's had to utilize my faith to get prayers answered. My faith and prayers have been used to pray for family members who have had surgery. She used her faith to stand in agreement with my brother, who has overcome the "C" Cancer through faith and belief. She's used her faith to help my sister overcome unforeseen legal matters. And most importantly, Yolanda has used my faith to overcome my own medical challenges.

I remember one instance where I was really struggling with my faith. I had just lost my job and my husband had been laid off a few months prior. We were struggling to make ends meet and I was starting to lose hope. I prayed and prayed, but it felt like my prayers were going unanswered. I decided to go to my church's prayer group and share my situation with them. They prayed with me and for me, and I felt my faith start to come back. A few days later, I got a call from a friend who told me about a job opening that was perfect for me. I ended up getting the job and everything worked out in the end.

If you are ever struggling with your faith, remember that you are not alone. There are people who care about you and are willing to help you through your struggles. Praying is a powerful way to connect with God and ask for His help. Don't give up hope, and keep your faith in the power of prayer.

Praying is a powerful way to connect with God and ask for His help. Keep faith in the power of prayer, and don't give up hope.

Faith prayers can help you overcome any obstacle. with God and to ask for His help. Don't give up hope, and keep faith in the power of prayer.

My faith has helped me overcome medical challenges that would have caused one to fold. The adversary attacked my body with breast cancer, but I refused to give in. I continued to pray and have faith, even when it was hard. My faith prayers were answered, and I am now cancer-free. This experience has taught me the power of prayer and the importance of never giving up hope.

If you are ever struggling with your faith, remember that you are not alone. There are people who care about you and who will help you through your faith journey. Praying is a powerful way to connect with God, and faith prayers can help you overcome any obstacle in life. No matter what challenges you are facing, don't give up hope. Remember that there is power in prayer, and keep faith in the unshakable power of God.

The adversary attacked my body with breast cancer, but I refused to give in. I continued to pray and have faith, even when it was hard. My faith prayers were answered, and I am now cancer-free. This experience has taught me the power of prayer and the importance of never giving up hope. If you are ever struggling with your faith, remember that you are not alone.

Then the adversary attacked my body covid, but I refused to give in. I continued to pray and have faith, even when it was hard. My faith prayers were answered, and I am now covid-free. This experience has taught me the power of prayer and the importance of never giving up hope. If you are ever struggling with your faith, remember that you are not alone. There are people who care about you and who will help you through your faith journey.

Praying is a powerful way to connect with God, and faith prayers can help you overcome any obstacle in life. No matter what challenges you are facing, don't give up hope. Remember that there is power in prayer, and keep faith in the unshakable power of God. Faith prayers Keywords: overcoming covid, unshakable faith, powerful prayer, never give up hope If you are ever struggling with your faith, remember that you are not alone.

It's been a little over three months since I signed up for Covid-19. I remember feeling so sick like I had the flu on steroids. My entire body ached; I had a fever and couldn't breathe. I thought for sure I was going to die.

Thankfully, I didn't. But recovering from Covid-19 has not been easy. People seem to think that you're all better once you're over the initial sickness. But that's just not the case.

I'm still dealing with the fatigue and brain fog daily. Simple tasks that used to be easy, like getting dressed or taking a shower, now take all the energy I have. And some days, I can barely. It's been a little over a month since I was diagnosed with Covid-19. I remember the day I found out like it was yesterday. I was at work and suddenly started feeling ill. A colleague of mine suggested I go home and rest, but I didn't want to leave work early. I thought maybe if I just powered through, I would feel better. But I knew something was wrong when I got home that evening. I had a headache, my body ached all over, and I couldn't stop shaking from the cold. The next day, I went to get tested, and sure enough, it came back positive for Covid-19.

The next few weeks were some of the hardest of my life. I was completely isolated from the outside world and felt very scared and alone. The virus hit me hard, and I wasn't sure if I would make it for a while. But with the support of my family and friends, I slowly started to get better.

It's been over a month now since I first got sick, and I'm happy to say that I'm finally on the mend. It's been a long and difficult road, but I'm grateful to be alive and to be able to share my story.

If there's one thing I've learned from this experience, it's that we are all stronger than we think. And no matter how hard things get, we can always overcome them.

If you or someone you know is struggling with Covid-19, I want you to know that you are not alone. There is hope, and there is help. Reach out to your friends and family for support, and don't be afraid to ask for help if you need it. We will get through this together. Now let's talk about living with lupus after overcoming Covid 19

I have struggled with autoimmune conditions all my life, and my family has a medical history of autoimmune conditions. During my late teenage years, I was diagnosed with ulcerative colitis, and in my 40s, I was diagnosed with an autoimmune, underactive thyroid during a bout of severe depression. I have always had unexplained rashes on my arms, face, and back that would come and go, mouth ulcers, and painful cracks at the sides of my mouth.

I also had issues with my lungs following a bad bout of whooping cough. My ANA reading was positive intermittently. I was sent to see a cardiologist who suspected an autoimmune connective tissue problem underlying my condition. He wanted me to see a rheumatologist.

The first rheumatologist I saw re-ran my blood tests at a different laboratory and some tests specifically for autoimmune conditions. The results came back largely normal. He said the previous laboratory had been "looking" for a positive result! I went away feeling that I needed to stop worrying about something wrong and get on with my life.

2021 was a very difficult year for my family. After a bout of Covid 19, the attending doctors got wind of my medical records with displayed records of a mass on my breast. I started at 6 months, and my adult daughter Son -In -Law and we were also going through some very hard times. My stress levels were very high, and I regularly cared for my granddaughter and others in my family. I began to feel very unwell, extremely fatigued, and awful pains all over my body but particularly bad in my lower back, hips, knees, and legs. I had a nasty rash on my back. I went to my GP, who ran a rheumatology blood test set. Again, my ANA came back at a relatively high level. She sent me off to see another rheumatologist as I didn't want to see the one, I had seen previously.

He ran all the blood tests again using a different lab, and this time my ANA was 1:2560, which is extremely high, and my double-stranded DNA was also positive.

He diagnosed Lupus and sent me away with a script for Plaquenil. At a subsequent visit, he added Amitriptyline which treats neuropathic pain which was preventing me from sleeping. These medications have helped significantly, and during 2017 my health improved greatly. I also began swimming laps in a heated pool a couple of days per week to ease the pain in my muscles and joints as well as improve my overall fitness.

Currently, I am mostly feeling well. I still have pain in my hips, knees, legs, and lower back. It is much better controlled, but I still need to take pain medication sometimes. I need to be careful with my stress levels as this is a very real factor in worsening my lupus symptoms.

I also try not to get overtired and to keep away from people with colds and flu, as I go down hard if I get an infection. A recent, very bad bout of flu saw me requiring prednisone to help with my breathing. The most important thing I learned from my Lupus journey is that I'm not bulletproof. I need to exercise real self-care, or I cannot care for my loved ones. This means I must sometimes say no and stop before exhaustion sets in. My husband and I have a deep Christian faith, and this gives us hope for the future, whatever that may bring.

I wish you all well with your own Lupus journeys.

The most important thing that I have learned from my Lupus journey is that I'm not bulletproof. I need to exercise real self-care, or I cannot care for my loved ones. This means I must sometimes say no and stop before exhaustion sets in. My husband and I have a deep Christian faith, and this gives us hope for the future, whatever that may bring. I wish you all well with your own Lupus journeys. Sometimes you might find yourself doubtful and wavering. It happens to us all.

Action Steps

1 Faith: If you don't waiver and stand in faith, your breakthrough will manifest. It's been a little over three months since I signed up for Covid-19. I remember feeling so sick like I had the flu on steroids. My entire body ached; I had a fever and couldn't breathe. I thought for sure I was going to die.

2: Not Alone

If you are ever struggling with your faith, remember that you are not alone. There are people who care about you and are willing to help you through your struggles. Praying is a powerful way to connect with God and ask for His help. Don't give up hope, and keep your faith in the power of prayer.

3: Persevere

People seem to think that you're all better once you're over the initial sickness. But that's just not the case. Recovering from Covid-19 has not been easy. You might feel like Covid dominates your entire world. It might be for a period. Keep the faith and follow medical advice and self-care.

Resources

FB: Yolanda Owens

Foffia2003@yahoo.com

ysolovesjesus@gmail.com

TOMIKO BALLANTYNE-NISBETT

Interrogating Sisterhood

Quote

"Greatness, Trinidadian style, was thrust upon me from the cradle."-
Eric Eustace Williams

Biography

Tomiko Ballantyne-Nisbett was born in the United States and raised in Trinidad and Tobago. In the twin-island republic, the food is better than the writing, and the writers have won Nobel Prizes (among other Neo-colonial forms of foolishness that we reify unnecessarily). Thus, the food always wins out, even for Tomiko, who loves to prepare Trinidadian food, mainly for herself.

She hustled as a freelance writer, professor, rubric expert, and scoring professional in this white supremacist world to pay off her student loans, and still wants everyone else to get theirs paid off by the government. In so doing, she happily demonstrates that she is not a hater and wants the best for all members of society, except, of course, monsters and the like. Of all entities in our universe, Tomiko loves her mother and her cat the most.

She loves documentaries, select sci-fi output, and almost all scary movies, good or bad. Within reason, Tomiko loves and supports everybody black.

My undergraduate alma mater, the illustrious Spelman College, has a ritual that most of us were apprehensive about taking part in. For formal occasions, we were to wear conservative white dresses with flesh-toned stockings, "sensible" black shoes, and very little jewelry. Every time. As freshmen, we wore this outfit to be welcomed into the sisterhood. If Maya Angelou or Johnetta B. Cole happened to be in town, we had to be scrubbed and ready in our weird nurse outfits. At graduation, we wore this getup under our gowns adorned with Kente stoles and light blue cords. And for the most part, everyone hated it.

The sensible black shoes were frustrating. Who wears close-toed black shoes with a white dress? How do these items go together? Wouldn't you be able to make it work with open-toed shoes so you could at least show off a pedicure? As undergraduates, we were all trying to look like fly black excellence and this tradition was really getting in the way of that possibility. But every girl who tried to get away with a skintight white bustier dress with bare legs and zebra print shoes was summarily stopped at the door and sent back to the dorms to change.

During freshman orientation, the elder members of the sisterhood explained to us that at the turn of the century, a conservative white dress was the way black women dressed up for formal occasions and that a pair of sensible black shoes were what most students could afford to wear. Sure, even in the year 1900 most women would have loved a pair of white shoes to go along with their white dresses. But what kind of investment was that for your average African-American woman in the 1900s? How would white shoes be kept clean, and how often would they be worn? The college could justify asking parents to send their daughters off to Atlanta with a pair of black close-toed shoes, but white shoes made no sense then, and they wanted us to consider that now.

They wanted us to physically engage with a tradition that might produce in us empathy for the sisters that came before us. While we complained that we were the last campus in Atlanta to get WiFi, our sisters before us had to fight with the administration to rock Afro hairstyles. While we fussed and carried on about the single room of blue plastic mats and old step aerobics equipment that constituted our "gym", our sisters before us were so oppressed under the weight of respectability politics that if they were seen being openly involved in the Civil Rights Movement, they risked expulsion. While Morehouse was constantly celebrated for its incredible legacy, the legacy of Morehouse students raping us and getting away with it loomed over our experience.

It was important, therefore, to find those moments of empathy and to think about the continued ways that the color of our skin defined our experiences. I spent my junior year of undergrad at the last remaining women's college at Oxford University, which was St. Hilda's College. And for the first time, I realized that the sisterhood that I'd been complaining about, the sisterhood I left, was the only true sisterhood I'd experienced beyond my own drama with my biological half-sister. Because at the end of the academic year at St. Hilda's, I sat in a crowded bar with friends while we drunkenly regaled each other with stories about the racist headmistress of the school, who was so outwardly and openly hostile to women of color.

That we found her laughable and worthy of our pity. With our strength in numbers, none of the 4 of us mentioned the various moments during the year that we'd caught each other one-on-one, sobbing in the stacks of the Bodleian Library.

Because the white women librarians refused to lend us books, wasting away and looking gaunt because none of the white women lunch ladies served us as much food as the others, scrounging around for cash because the white headmistress insisted that we didn't need much money from our home institutions, being denied canoes to go punting on the river Thames because, as a more senior girl in another college argued, "They don't like black people in their boats".

Not to mention trying to find your shade of makeup in Boots drugstore with no assistance from the white women shop workers, or being followed around by yet more white women while you looking for warm socks in Selfridges. And when we finally got the hang of the local club system and created a safe space for ourselves, our parties were discovered by white girls who wanted to know why we suddenly seemed to be having a good time, only to be broken up by authorities who wanted to know where all the white women were going.

I was easily the worst adjusted of anyone at Oxford because all the other black women exchange students from America were accustomed to the silencing, shaming, sidelining, ignoring, and in some cases tyranny and villainy of white women. I'd experienced it in high school of course, but living with these women in dorms was a different life completely.

I would be horrified at the way my hair was touched and my behind was grabbed but the 3 remaining black women insisted that white American women were much worse. In fact, by the end of the year when a white woman did or said something offensive to one of us in a Tesco or in line at the bank, people stopped telling me about these situations entirely. Watching the 7 stages of grief play out on my face was amusing at first, but eventually hard to take.

For the entire academic year, we of course said nothing about the fact that some of our greatest white women tormentors dated black men who wouldn't so much as a fart on us. We never once discussed that. That story required no unpacking.

I wondered then as I wondered now — why did Spelman spend so much time hammering the idea of sisterhood into us while St. Hilda's made no mention and blithely ignored the lack of sisterhood? What was more important to St. Hilda's than that? The answer, of course, is whiteness. James Baldwin once argued that black people have endured racism by [dismissing] white people as the "slightly mad victims of their own brainwashing." As black people, we all know that the lure of whiteness and the call of its power has always been and will always be more important than any other social construct.

When the owner of IT Cosmetics sold her company to Revlon for a billion dollars several years ago and then touted it as a major step forward for "diversity" because she is a full-figured woman in an industry of toothpicks, it is not enough to celebrate her for her achievements when, as all women of color know, IT Cosmetics has yet to make a makeup shade for black women to wear, aside from two colors that are clearly shades that were mixed for white women with darkening agents added in.

We know this because when we apply said makeup, we look casket-sharp and funeral ready. This company's bold-faced racist practices cannot be swept under the rug as they co-opt the language of diversity that BIPOC has fought for, for we all know that a plus-sized woman of color is treated far worse by society than a plus-sized white woman.

Just as Claudette Colvin was erased from the discussion of the Montgomery Bus Boycotts for being dark-skinned and pregnant, I see the coming erasure of Tarana Burke from Me Too. Sure, she is continuing to do important work for the movement and there is always the possibility that she eschews notoriety in favor of the work, but who benefitted more from accompanying her to the 2018 Golden Globe Awards, Tarana Burke, or the white woman actress Michelle Williams who toted her along to the festivities?

As noted white feminist Madeline Davies has argued, "Throughout the history of feminism, we white women have continually focused the movement on our equal pay, our marriages, and our reproductive rights—only demanding alliances when it suits us and failing to show up and fight when it does not....We comfort ourselves with the notion that we are not as bad as white men.

[We] lie to ourselves about the myriad of ways that we have profited from and advanced white supremacy. It's hard to be introspective and admit that you've had a hand in another's oppression, to face the terrifying notion of change and the relinquishing of social power, when instead you can hide behind your own victimhood. Self-pity can serve as a means of absolution, a balm that convinces us that, because we too are victims of white supremacist patriarchy, we couldn't possibly be oppressors."

It is incredibly brave for white women to come out and describe their experiences of sexual assault and harassment, but for women of color, such bravery comes with half the credit, and Harvey Weinstein only issued public statements denying that anything ever happened to you, Salma Hayek, and you, Lupita Nyongo, while remaining mum about most other assaults. It is possible to be Lena Dunham or Tina Fey, two white women who are celebrated for their feminist advancements, whose entertainment programs and whose own statements belie a possible disdain for women of color that hardly any white people notice.

It is worth noting that in this instance, we should also not deny bigotry against queer women, women with disabilities, and women who are white-presenting in the world who are not actually white people. To deny that bigotry would be negligent and oppressive by itself. But before you congratulate yourselves for marching and protesting against the oddly large number of white male pedophiles running for elected office, remember to use the language and tools that feminism provides to uplift those who are victimized, and do not use this as an excuse to complain about a sisterhood being "divided".

For it is not enough to assume the existence of a sisterhood without doing the work to dismantle the white supremacist tyranny that prevents your sisters of color from experiencing said sisterhood. Ignoring racism in your universe does nothing to destroy it. Furthermore, it is not fair to your sisters of color to leave the entire burden of intersectionality on their laps. You can thank Margaret Sanger for her scientific interventions but you must not add her racist eugenicist impulses as a mere footnote.

You must teach the Combahee River Collective Statement alongside your hallowed dissections of The Feminine Mystique. If women of color are singing a song that addresses this political moment, let us value that voice. Saying2 "keep your BIPOC politics out of entertainment" is like saying I want to benefit from your experiences as a person of color without having to consider the tragedy behind those experiences.

Consider the possibility that many women of color turn on the TV during the annual women's march and can't help but laugh, considering that statistically, there is a strong possibility that many of the women in vagina hats are being handed cups of coffee by the same police that would kill us at the first opportunity voted for the Donald Trumps and Roy Moores of the world.

These daughters and granddaughters of Women's Lib voted for a man who boasted about grabbing people's vaginas, while we daughters and granddaughters of Spelman College wear close-toed black shoes to try to invoke the struggle of women before us.

This is the time when, as a black woman, I have insisted upon preserving my own health and strength in the face of the foolishness we encounter on a daily basis from the pantheon of pink "girl boss" energy that pervades the culture we currently find ourselves in. My prescription has been to minimize drama and stress by minimizing dramatic and stressful situations that are unwarranted with regard to earning an income.

The best way to cope with the situation we currently and eternally find ourselves in is to remember that the long durée of history will absolve us, as it always does. Black women are always the infographic that other women use to craft their aesthetic, and we always will be. Just as our ancestors coped by calling out the nonsense alongside laughing with their sisters, so will we. And this is how we honor the women who wore close-toed shoes, doing what they had to do until there could be a generation of women who come ever closer to doing what they want to do.

We will not live to see the end of this white supremacist hellscape, but we can certainly find ways to manage the stress it foists upon us, and we can ultimately do that by taking care of one another in the interiority of blackness. That look you share with another black woman in public that requires no conversation or unpacking is a tender moment that no one else was invited to except other black women who know that in that look, we had an entire meeting and discussed a whole season of white supremacist nonsense.

If we focus on being grateful for those wordless meetings in difficult times, we will continue to have them, and they will continue to strengthen us.

Action Steps

Listen to your body and give it mostly what it needs, and a little bit of what it wants.

1. Yoga — I am hesitant to recommend a yoga teacher because I strongly recommend clicking around on YouTube until you find someone you like whose body type represents what you currently have going on, as opposed to what you wish you were.

2. Marijuana — If you're not a smoker or an edible/drinkable person, try the THC body lotions that are permeating the market these days. They're great for menstrual pains.

3. Book Club — Start your own with your home girl who has a Zoom subscription, and make sure you vary the subject matter based on tastes. Read outside of your comfort zone. Push yourself to try something different.

Resource

mikoism@gmail.com

72

CANDACE LEWIS

Let's Take a Walk, My Child

·· 73 ··

Quote

"See the joy, Be the joy, Bring the JOY."

Biography

Candace Lewis is a proud mother of 4 and grandmother of 5 which they call her CaCa. She is a successful nurse of 29 years and has enjoyed caring for others throughout several states and in a variety of different areas in nursing. Now Candace is caring for others through her writing.

Her vision and goals are to help people with healing in their souls. She also plans to run and operate domestic violence shelters for both males and females that will provide service to help with healing, educate and promote that trusting in God and surrendering to his will, any, and everything for the great is possible.

Let's take a walk, My Child; it's a bright, bright, sunny day. It's Sunday!!! CANDY, it is time to get up now! I can recall my mother singing out early on Sunday mornings. At a very young age, I remember going to church with my grandparents or mother. On Saturday night, we would prepare for church the next day, which mainly consisted of washing and getting our hair pressed with that very hot, hot comb. You know the one that seems to burn your ear, but that was just the grease popping. I wrapped my hair to make sure I did not get it wet when I took a bath and laid out my clothes.

It was boring and quiet when I went to church with my paternal grandmother. My grandmother would have church snacks for me, those orange spongy candies, soft peppermint balls, or raisins. Church didn't last long there. I can remember going to a Baptist church with my mother and maternal grandmother. I would see one or the other cry sometimes, there was a choir, clapping, the preacher was louder, and the church held just a little bit longer. At times my paternal grandfather would go to Mass, Candy do you want to go?

My Aunt was only 6 years older than me, so she was like a big sister, and I would just follow her. We would put our bikes away and jump in the car with grandpa with our outside clothes on and as I viewed it, we yodeled that's what I saw Catholics singing, said a prayer, and was out. Of course, at that young age, I didn't learn anything about God. At the age of 5, my father began to seek a relationship with God to help save him from losing his family. My mother planned to move the 2 of us out of town, leaving him behind. My father is a biker and at that time, he hung out at a Harley Davidson spot, sharing with someone his troubles at home; this man invited him to Bible Class. My father accepted and we began to go to Bible Class.

The congregation was majority Caucasian, and very quiet. I would go with the children and do biblical arts and crafts. At this time, my father has decided to further his spiritual journey.

Wow, this church is pretty and fancy. My parents found a church home. There are fancy lights, the lights will be dimmed, and there will be lights in the ceiling in the shape of a cross. It was a lot of singing, clapping, and dancing around. The choir was loud and joyful, and the preacher was loud, but the church held for a long time. My father decided to get baptized and if memory serves correct, I believe it was under the baptism of the trilogy, Father, Son, and the Holy Spirit. At that time, the church just wowed me, the baptism pool was in the ground, and you entered going down spiral stairs and stepping into the pool.

At this church, there wasn't a children's church or a place for biblical arts and crafts. Children were always present in the sanctuary. I remember the spirit would be high and all the people that would be in the prayer line, and at times, some would even fall out. In due time, my father felt like he was missing something spiritually, so a church member whom my parents had befriended took me to visit an apostolic faith church. At the end of that service, my parents were both baptized in Jesus' name.

We are saved; my parents rejoice as they receive the pressure gift of the Holy Ghost after being placed on their knees and utter Hallelujah until they begin to speak in tongues. That was the practice for sanctified churches. This was in the year 1974; my parents were saved, my father saved his marriage, and they have a new church home. We attended church Wednesday, bible class, Friday saints meeting, Saturday if you were in the choir, and Sunday consisted of, Sunday School, Sunday morning service, and Sunday evening joy night. As far as practicing faith and understanding and believing, as I think back, I didn't have a clue what was going on. The adult beliefs were forced upon the children and teens. No wearing pants, no jewelry, no circular music, no t.v. and the list goes on.

My parents didn't abide by all the beliefs that were taught at this church, so as I aged, I had a little bit more freedom than my church friends. My church friends were more like family because you spent more time with them than your blood family. There was a nursery setting there, but I had outgrown that setting, so there were many of us children and teens in the sanctuary. We did have a Jr Church with a Jr choir that met up on Sunday evenings before joy night service.

I can remember being taught Jesus is the son of God, and this church did not believe in the trilogy. As I aged and reached my teenage years. I have a little understanding of prayer and faith. Quarterly our Bishop would call a 3-day fast. No food from Wednesday morning until Friday at 4 pm. After the fast is completed, that Friday night, there would be foot washing and communion. One Sunday night, I was 8 years old and decided to get baptized, so thereafter, I would participate in communion and foot washing.

Now I understand, fast, pray, believe, and wait. That's it. That's easy to do when you want something. At age 14, I fought through my first 3-day fast. I wanted a new moped. I didn't get it. I did think maybe God will give me something else. During that time, I was preparing for the cheerleading team for 11th grade. I practiced and stretched months before tryouts, and I fasted. This time, it worked; I made the cheerleading team. At times as a teenager, the spirit would hit me; I would shout and begin to utter tongues. I didn't understand what that meant, I just knew now I have the Holy Ghost but sinned.

As an adult, to the best of my ability, I worked on trying to attend church on Sunday mornings. When I was in my twenties, I was into, as folk say, sex, drugs, and rock n roll. I would continue to go to church, maybe not as consistent, but I thought that was having a relationship with God. I have stepped into darker darkness, adultery, fornication, and homosexuality. I would ask myself, why am I like this? I grew up in church, and over time, my father was called to preach, so I am a preacher's kid. Yeah, Yeah, we are the worst.

I had proven that to be true in a sense; I became pregnant at seventeen and married right on my eighteenth birthday. As time moved on, I began to feel darker on the inside, but in other areas, I was happy. I was a teenage mother; I obtained my LPN and made a decent income to support my family, but somewhere deep inside, something wasn't right. At the beginning of my forties, I decided to cross back over the fence to heterosexuality. That was challenging spiritually and prior to that decision, I had suffered from a mental breakdown and depression. At some point, all I could do is call out to God, with little understanding, just fast, pray, have faith, and wait. My soul couldn't wait any longer.

Let's shut me down. A close friend of mine introduced me to reading motivational and self-improvement books. I took a long time out to do some soul-searching. I had not been to church in a couple of years, but I continued to pray, have faith, and wait. What I began to learn is that I need to have a connection with

God. I need to communicate with him. At forty-seven years old, my soul was weary, I had gotten injured at my job, could not work, was homeless, and lost it all.

During that time, I joined a church and called myself saved until I bounced back and went out the window for a few years. As I mentioned forty-seven, I'm feeling lost. I went to New Year's Eve service in 1986 and again, I'm saved for just a short period of time. I began to think, why do I get saved, throw it away, and repeat this cycle? What am I missing? I began to have the mindset to forget my salvation. I don't even know if there is a heaven or hell. Is what I'm being told the truth? I'm not going to anyone else's church.

God saw otherwise. In 2018 I was injured at work again, cannot work, and depression sets in deeper because it never went away from prior years. I'm experiencing a lot of sin, which I know better, and I'm beginning to feel bad. In 2019 my baby girl invited me to church, and I will keep going. Now this time around, I didn't say I'm saved; I really asked God, how do I get this right? He answered, just get to know me openly.

Come to me with all your mess and lay your burdens down; I will take care of the rest. I thought I'd been doing that by fasting, praying, faith, and waiting. I was beginning to think God said I was too bad, and he can't help me because I keep reneging on the deals I make.

God is the one with the promises! I realized I can't make God any promises or offer any deals. I have a church home; our shepherd is really a great teacher and I'm beginning to understand this spiritual walk. My first move, take notes at church, write down scriptures, go back and read them and ask God for understanding. The second move is to pay attention to my soul. My soul means more than my body; that's forever; this body isn't. I realize I need to heal my soul, past and present. I pull out tools I have gained along the way and stored them up, but now it's time to pull them out. Go to church and be part of the church, not just in attendance.

I sat in the second row from the front, my attendance was consistent with Sunday morning worship and Thursday Bible class and was on time due to riding with my daughter, bless her heart, she had my back. I began to journal again, take time out daily to pray, and listen to gospel music. At times I'm still battling feeling good or bad in my soul. I didn't give up. I pulled out more tools and started back reading, but now more spiritual books. I learned to meditate on God and that was the key for me.

2021, I really surrendered; I got it finally. My mindset had changed, my soul was happy, and God began to bring people into my life to assist in my healing and flourishing. I finally really understood, I am a child of God; he takes me as I am as long as I reach out and believe. But it's work that must be done. I found out fasting and praying wasn't just that. I had to prove myself to God by being obedient. I learned to talk to him, be transparent with God, let him know my weaknesses, and the more I give him attention and put him first, the better I feel.

I found out the devil doesn't like this new mindset, this new way of thinking and carrying myself. From time to time, I would slip, but I learned God is merciful, therefore he gave his only begotten son for our sins.

I thought I don't think it was fair as I would sin a little and think it was ok; God gave his son. With the relationship I had built with God, I felt in my soul more and more that this is not the way it works, but you're on the right track and we will get you better. I began to understand the meaning of wearing your armor daily. God, how do I do that?

I got a spiritual life coach, and my God sister started a book club, and this opened my heart more to understanding my armor. What was a big learning for me was recognizing the devil and learning his strategies? I learned there are many different satanic spirits the devil will throw your way. He will find your weakest link and attempt to break you at any given time. Now I have a relationship with God, I'm learning more and more now how to communicate and listen to him. I'm learning to toughen my armor daily, by staying in the word and giving God time every day.

Pay attention to those spirits and watch what you consume, and surround yourself spiritually and mentally. I am aware it takes work and at times, it is challenging because the devil will show his face when he feels like he has lost you. During those challenging times when the devil is riding my back, I know it is a spirit that can be rebuked and the more you resist, he will flee. During my resisting moments, I am growing, so now my going back to the worldly ways, I don't see my future. I finally learned why every time I would say I'm saved and would throw the save out the window and couldn't get it right. Those were demons I was fighting for years.

At the beginning of my story, I would mention, children were present in the sanctuary. I believe at times, during prayer, satanic spirits being prayed out of an adult could have jumped onto children. I am not a bad person, as I used to think, I've been fighting spirits! To conclude, my belief has changed; no more just fast, pray, faith, and wait. I now clearly understand that faith without work equals death.

My belief has changed; no more just fast, prayer, faith and wait. I now clearly understand that faith without work equals death. You can as well. Take the step and give yourself to God.

Action Steps

1: Standing on your faith

Now I understand, fast, pray, believe, and wait. That's it. That's easy to do when you want something. At age 14, I fought through my first 3-day fast. I wanted a new moped. I didn't get it. I did think maybe God will give me something else. During that time, I was preparing for the cheerleading team for 11th grade. I practiced and stretched months before tryouts, and I fasted. This time, it worked; I made the cheerleading team. At times as a teenager, the spirit would hit me, I would shout and begin to utter in tongues. I didn't understand what that meant, I just knew now I have the Holy Ghost but sinned.

2: Give Oneself up.

I got a spiritual life coach, and my God sister started a book club, and this opened my heart more to understanding my armor. What was a big learning for me was recognizing the devil and learning his strategies? I learned there are many different satanic spirits the devil will throw your way. He will find your weakest link and attempt to break you at any given time. Now I have a relationship with God, I'm learning more and more now how to communicate and listen to him. I'm learning to toughen my armor daily, by staying in the word and giving God time every day. Pay attention to those spirits and watch what you consume, and surround yourself spiritually and mentally. I am *aware it takes work and at times, it is challenging because the devil will show his face when he feels like he has lost you.*

3: Spiritual Growth: Say No to the world and yes to God.

My belief has changed; no more just fast, pray, faith, and wait. I now clearly understand that faith without work equals death. I am growing, so now I'm going back to the worldly ways; I don't see my future. I finally learned why every time I would say I'm saved and would throw the save out the window and couldn't get it right.

Those were demons I was fighting for years. At the beginning of my story, I would mention, children were present in the sanctuary. I believe at times, during prayer, satanic spirits being prayed out of an adult could have jumped onto children. I am not a bad person, as I used to think, I've been fighting spirits!

Resources

Candyly4@yahoo.com

TIFFANY HOLLINS-MOSS
Worth The Fight

Quote

"*Know who you are show the rest.*"

Biography

Tiffany Hollins-Moss is an extraordinary 39-year-old Wife, Mother of 3, and School nurse in the Hillsborough County School District. She has always been a voracious learner and teacher. Known for inspiring others through Imparting wisdom to push through and achieve greatness.

Tiffany is passionate about empowering others and has learned the best form of teaching is by example. Over time Tiffany became an unintentional motivational speaker. Now walking in her power and with intention Tiffany, as a first-time author is using her voice and platforms to drive the mission to Empower and Motivate you to reach your goals. Remember and understand that the past you lived through, will never decide your future. You and you alone control the outcome.

-

-

At 35 years old, I sat on my little sister's couch crying. Literally, it's 2:30 in the morning and here I am a grown woman crying while I scroll through Instagram. See 12 hrs. earlier I received a call "Don't ask any questions, just pack a bag and get here. Your sister needs you. "By 6 pm I was boarding, with my 2-year-old son, a flight back home to NY. While on that flight I kept thinking about checking my email.

You see, 3 months prior I had applied to nurse school and was accepted. The only problem was, Registration was in 3 days, and I knew there was no way I would get back in time. Once again, I had put on my cape to fight someone else's battle. My wants and needs are damned, I was coming to the rescue. As I sat there crying, angry at myself, once again for giving up on myself when I came across a video.

This Video was of a young man, using a robotic walking machine, saying "when I got shot, they said I would never walk again, I am proving them wrong daily". Here he was with everything stacked against him, yet he didn't allow life and circumstances to stop him. Here I was getting in my own way. Baby this was a vicious cycle I had been re-running for over 10 years.

So, I had the decision to make, sit here and cry or fight for myself. See as "the bully beater" as I was affectionately known I could take on any battle and come out triumphant like David over Goliath, but only when I was fighting for everyone else. I never felt I was worth or could be worth fighting for. So, the next morning I humbled myself and called the dean, as I cried and explained the situation, she stopped me and said, "I am sorry I cannot hold your spot, but I do have a registration coming up in February for the night class, it will take 18 months, instead of 12, and it's at night."

I was crushed, night school was not the plan, I needed days. I decided at that moment that my dream and goal were worth fighting for, and any obstacle to my greatness would be slain in sight.

So, the day finally comes May 7th, 2018, I am starting nursing school. By this time, I am fired up. I found out that the highest honors in nursing school were the honor society and having the highest grades could land you the title of the mistress of ceremony, and those honors would belong to me, and me alone.

As with the first day of school, we engaged in some icebreakers. The most memorable were 3 questions that were asked. So, I answer all three questions, what is your greatest accomplishment? What is your goal? What are you willing to sacrifice to be here?

Well, this was easy, I had been discussing these things with myself daily. So, I was one of the first ones to finish writing, and she began going around asking people to say their answers out loud. Now, I have not been the most self-confident, nor the most transparent. Yet in this, I had to come as my raw, unfiltered self. So, she calls on me, and I don't hesitate.... My greatest accomplishment and proudest moment were overcoming suicidal thoughts. Yet at the age of 30, I finally desired to live for my children. My goal is, come graduation day no name called will be higher than my own, I will make the honor society, and be mistress of ceremony. What am I willing to sacrifice, everything?

The teachers' response was shocking. That's an overconfident thing to say, don't you think you're aiming too high?

Well as you all know when we really set our mind to something, life will test our resolve and dedication. Within a month I realized that night school was going to be more of a challenge than I could handle. See at the time my family's schedules were out of whack, which was fine because as a mom I was flexible. Yet this made my 16 yr. Old give up her passion for basketball to be able to pick up her brother from school until I got home at 10:30 pm four nights a week. This she did with no complaint, yet I felt guilty. When talking to that same little sister whose side I flew to many times, she says to me, "Sis, I have watched you sacrifice everything for everyone for so long, I want to see you have this for you. Send me my nephew; I got him; you go be great sis."

That day was the first of many sacrifices I had to make to achieve my dream. I even had to ask myself, was my dream worth fighting this hard for?

Within two weeks of sending my only son, my baby boy, to his aunt, my teacher showed her true colors. She began trying to break our class, with a special pleasure in knocking me down a peg. From belittling me for asking the question," You have no right to be asking questions; you have the highest grade on the exam." To tell me in front of the whole class to kill myself. It was not a healthy, encouraging environment. Through it all, I had to remind myself that this was my dream.

I remember crying after class, and my classmates, who were angry about her actions directed at us all, were now telling me that I was overreacting to her direct attacks. I tried going to the administration for help and was told in a meeting that if I complained again, I would be put on behavioral probation.

The problem with that is that ANY probation disqualifies you for the mistress of ceremony. So now, as I am already suffering from being disconnected from all 3 of my children, now I must take verbal and mental abuse. Yet, I did say I was willing to sacrifice everything. So, I isolated and silently fought harder. When that didn't stop me, I lived through multiple illnesses, having emergency surgery, and even losing my insurance, so I could not attend my therapy sessions.

For Tiffany, that would have been too much, but for the bully-beater, it was all in stride for the bully-beater. Even after the surgery, when I could not attend clinicals, the same teacher refused to assist with getting make-up clinical days. Working to produce fraudulent paperwork to try to steal my dream. Yet through it, the universe worked with me. See, class started at 4:30 pm, So I took advantage of the federal work-study program. I began to work with the new daytime administration daily from 7:30 am-4 pm.

My work ethic and dedication put me in a position to have the ear of the man in charge. He jumped in and took over when I asked how to secure my makeup clinical dates. Wow, someone else fought for me. Maybe I am worth it.

The rest of the journey came with more heartbreak and mental pain. On April 1st, I rushed my grandfather to the hospital.

I would spend the following month going to class and working. Yet my mind and heart were still in the hospital room with my granddad. Each weekend I returned to the hospital to care for him. As the month progressed, I began to second guess his care, so I had him give consent for me to discuss his care in depth with his care team.

On April 26, it was determined that there was nothing they could do for him. Yet I was the one who had to relay this to him and our family. We had two options, wait it out and watch him suffer, or choose to go into surgery that he won't live through.

On that day, I did the hardest thing. I called all of our family to relay, "Come love on him and say goodbye; he wants to go .... On his terms. On Monday evening, we had our final conversation. His last word to me was, "You are damn good at what you do, do NOT quit."

Tuesday morning, he went into surgery and made it out alive. I breathed with uncertainty.... What will his life be like now? Wednesday, May 1st, I finally got to my first day of 6 am makeup clinical, only to receive the call that my grandfather, who I loved dearly, had transitioned at 5:30 that morning.

The fight must go on. So, with tears in my eyes, I continue to fight for my dream.

By the last six months of class, I was sailing. Seeing that I doubled down on my dream, it became harder for the teacher and much of the outside world to affect me for more than a few moments. Those same classmates were now back to crying and complaining daily about this same teacher and the actions they had endured and witnessed me overcome. See, this time, instead of fighting other battles. In doing so, I helped myself and the others that came after me. The teacher was forced into an early retirement... but that's a longer story for another day.

Through it all, I fought, cried, and even doubted myself and my dream a few times. Ultimately, on December 19, 2019. I stood on that stage and welcomed our families and friends to our pinning as the Mistress of ceremony.

At times in life, we often feel like giving up, giving in, and quitting. Please know and understand that some of the hardest battles you fight will be the ones that alter the course of your life.

I proudly tell my story to inspire you, and other women you love. The moments that it seems there is no way you can go on, know that your ancestors are encouraging. Remind yourself of the stories of other successful women, the ones who did not accept the word NO. Let this give you the courage to be your greatest self.

When it seems like life is throwing every possible obstacle and distraction in your path, I say.... Pick up speed and jump!! Head first into your dreams and goals. You will stumble, and you may even get bumps and bruises. Just like riding a bike, those falls make the success of completion so very much sweeter. With this I say to you, you are worth fighting for, but until you decide to pick up the sword, life will always win.

Action Steps

1. Love yourself, and decide to dream

Why do they need to do this?

Often when we dream about life, it's for the ones we love. Now I need you to take time and love yourself, in the way you love others. Allow yourself to dream what your most extraordinary life could look like. Be unapologetically optimistic. If you want that 8-bedroom home with the land, envision it. You want to be an incredible stay-at-home mom, with the time and resources to have a phenomenal existence. See it. Ultimately, you must love yourself and know that you are worthy of it all, to even begin to execute your goals.

2.   Commit to your dream and reaffirm your worth.

Why do they need to do this? Take time, write down and plan what you want. See your end goal and affirm what YOU want, not what you think others say you deserve, not what others have said you should want or have. Remind yourself daily of how great and capable you are.

Yes, you will have bad days, hard days, and discouraging days. It is on those days that you must dig deeper, reach into your depths, and pull all the strength and love you pour into others.

Visualize the part of YOU that needs it and pour it into yourself without measure. Unashamed and without apology.

3.   Allow flexibility, but commit to achievement, the greatest form of self-love

Why do they need to do this? Life is going to flow and change in every way possible. KNOW THIS and ACCEPT THIS. Success and empowerment are knowing that the only thing or person we can control is ourselves. Even if that means accepting where you are is just a step, not the destination.

In the end, life will live; it is up to you to love yourself, your goals, and your dreams for your legacy that allows you to be flexible enough to work around and through the trials and tribulations. Committing to you and your journey is the highest, most beautiful, and most valuable form of self-love.... Even more valuable than that Birkin bag or those Diamonds you desire.

Resources

nursetiffany1226@gmail.com

DR. LASHONE GARTH
Living My Best Life

Quote

"There's nothing I can't do, just things I haven't done yet."

Biography

Dr. LaShone Garth grew up in Detroit, Michigan, and started her journey in the military, enlisting at the age of 17. After spending four years on Active Duty, she left the service, entered the Georgia Army National Guard, went to Officer Candidate School, and was commissioned as a 2nd Lieutenant Military Police Officer.

LaShone spent eight years in the Guard before transitioning to the U.S. Army Reserve, where she honorably served the remainder of her 20-plus years, including a duty tour in the Iraq combat zone. She retired in 2013 with the rank of Major. After retiring, she served as an Assistant Professor of Military Science teaching leadership at Clemson University, the first African American woman selected for this position.

In 2015, she founded Blanket of Freedom, a nonprofit that supports veterans living with mental illness through the arts. She was named Woman of the Year by the National Association of Professional Women for her excellence and professionalism in business, and she was also honored by Rolling Out Magazine as one of the top 25 Women to know in Atlanta.

LaShone graduated with a BA in Psychology from Georgia State University and a MA in Forensic Psychology from The Chicago School of Professional Psychology. In December 2020, she earned her Doctorate in Social work from the University of Southern California and earned her place in the National Honor Society. She has held numerous leadership positions that include being a past National President of Sigma Phi Psi Sorority, Incorporated, the first sorority for United States Armed Forces Women and she is a proud member of the Illustrious Sisterhood of Delta Sigma Theta Sorority, Incorporated.

She is a former Ms. American Elegance Lady 2016, former Ms. Georgia American Elegance Lady 2015, Mrs. Atlanta 2014, and Mrs. Gwinnett County 2012. She also works tirelessly with and for military veterans.

LaShone is an accomplished model and actress with credits in TV, theater, and film. LaShone has started a self-titled production company, LGarth Productions, LLC, which opened up the door for her to gain honors as an award-winning writer and producer.

She has been coined as an up-and-coming producer and writer by C-magazine and Spaced-Out Magazine. She is currently producing her first full-feature film. LaShone is married to her husband, Casey, and resides in Atlanta, Georgia.

We all have aspirations to be successful and get all the things we desire, and live our best lives. As we know, life does not always work out the way we plan or hope. There's an old quote, "If you want to make God laugh, tell Him about YOUR plans." Even our best-laid plans can fall short of success. The goal is to find God's purpose for you and then move. The Word tells us, "Trust in the Lord with all thine heart; and lean not unto thine own understanding. "In all thy ways acknowledge him, and he shall direct thy paths." (Proverbs 3:5-6).

As the title of this chapter suggests, I am currently living my best life, however, it has not always been that way. It used to be "living my best LIE".

I've definitely had my share of ups and downs and I can definitely tell you that when I say down, I mean down. I was in a very dark place at one point in my life to the extent that I attempted to take my own life.

I woke up one morning and it was just like any other morning. I got up brushed my teeth, washed my face, and then stepped into my closet, grabbed one of my leather belts, wrapped it around my neck, and attempted to hang myself. Well, obviously it didn't work because I'm here now writing to you. It wasn't for lack of trying the only thing that saved me, outside of the heavenly father of course, is my weight. I was too heavy for the belt and for the closet rack and everything came crashing down around me. So, as I'm sitting there on the floor of the closet covered in clothes and shoes trying to figure out where my life was headed, I instantly knew what I had to do. I really believe that God spoke to me that day and told me that I had a mission that even I wasn't aware of. The end suddenly became the beginning of who I was to become and who I am today.

I was born in Detroit, Michigan to two loving parents. I was raised in church as a preacher's kid. Yes, my dad was a minister, Pastor, Reverend, or whatever terminology you'd like to use.

As you can imagine growing up as a preacher's kid, I had the tendency to be rebellious. That caused a lot of growing pains, to say the least. My life was definitely not traditional. My mom and dad were not married until I was about four years old. There were also often financial issues that caused us to move around frequently. It was still a loving household and I believe that my parents did everything they could to supply my needs.

Seven years later, my brother was born and it was just me, him, and my parents. Unfortunately, my parents divorced and my mom remarried and moved to California with her new husband and had three more children.

My brother and I stayed in Michigan temporarily so that I could finish high school and not have to be uprooted and so my brother still had some stability. During that time, we stayed with our Godmother, my Mom's best friend, and my Mom would visit as much as possible. As a young and impressionable girl, I didn't fare well without my Mom and was always engaging in risky behavior. I lost my virginity young and almost didn't graduate from high school.

Eventually, after trying to sell drugs and just making my father totally miserable he decided that he'd ship me off to the Army, which he did. When I left Michigan, my brother moved to California to be with my mother.

I harbored some feelings of guilt for leaving him but hoped that he would still thrive in California.

My Army experience, in the beginning, was less than desirable. Basically, I hated it but I knew that I didn't have other options at that time, so I dealt with it and I ended up retiring after a little over 20 years. So, I guess it worked out if you want to look at it that way. I had a series of failed marriages, 4 to be exact, and I really didn't know what I wanted to do with my life. Believe it or not, I even stripped for a few years.

Obviously not one of my greater moments. But I will say that the experience taught me a lot. I've learned how to accept every part of me, and Cameron (my stripper's name) is a part of me. Although a rebellious teenager, I was always academically gifted. I decided to go forward with my education. It wasn't an easy road. I took out tons of student loans and raked up over $200K of debt. Finally, I was able to finish my doctorate degree in social work from the University of Southern California.

So, what do I mean by living my best lie? Well, let me start from what I'll call the beginning of the end. During my last few years in the military, I had the opportunity, or so I thought at the time, to do a tour of duty in Iraq. It was an exciting time but also a very scary time. If you know anything about the war in Iraq and

Afghanistan, the United States suffered a lot of casualties. I went to Iraq from 2006 to 2007.

It was a life-changing experience. Looking back, I believe I was meant to go over there. I met my last and final husband in Iraq, and we've been married now for 15 years. This is actually the longest marriage I've ever had. Even all my previous marriages combined don't add up to 15 years which is kind of funny but I digress. Being over in Iraq gave me a different perspective on life because I learned that life is short and fleeting.

If you don't use the time given to you on this earth wisely, you'll end up at the end of life on your deathbed with regrets. Life in another country can be really different, especially in countries that are at war. I had constant anxiety and was always hypervigilant and it definitely took a toll on me. Stress also came from the actual job I had to do over there. I was the first one to fill the position that I went over there for so there wasn't really a blueprint for what I was supposed to do. I felt like a deer in headlights. Can you say imposter syndrome? I was so lost. However, after a couple of months, I got in my groove and was able to make the job my own, and my work was recognized and set the stage for all who followed me.

When I left, my husband had to remain there for another 15 months. The thought of him being over there, possibly in danger, added to my anxiety level. When I got back home, I tried to get back into regular life and I continued to lie to myself that everything was ok, that I was ok, but the truth is that I wasn't.

I had a life-changing experience that caused me to go into a very deep depression. I wasn't sleeping, I gained a lot of weight, and I was in a lot of pain emotionally and physically. The military can take a lot of you. I not only had a broken mind but a broken body. Ask any veteran what military doctors prescribe no matter what the ailment. Motrin, 800mg, the cure all.

Well, it didn't cure anything and I just continued to slip deeper and deeper into despair. Sure, I was able to function but my face was a mask of lies. I stopped enjoying life. I couldn't even really enjoy my marriage and it was the best one I ever had! My outlet used to be working out but I was in so much mental and physical pain that working out became a challenge. My husband was really concerned and I could tell that he felt hopeless, so I would just tell him I was alright. Before retirement, I tried to seek counseling but again, the military fell short. Eventually, I found myself on the closet floor.

So how did I get to my best life, you ask? Living your best life doesn't mean that you have everything in order or that you have everything together. As a matter of fact, it can be the exact opposite. So, I definitely don't want you to believe that that's what I mean when I say that. That morning while sitting in my closet I got a word from God and he told me that I wasn't alone. He told me that others could be saved by experience

He birthed in me the foundation for my non-profit, Blanket of Freedom, Inc. I founded this organization to help veterans cope with mental illness through the arts in an effort to stop veteran suicide. I dove in head first. I began writing movies, television shows, and plays. Getting as many of my veteran friends involved. Blanket of Freedom is still in its infancy but the goal is to offer counseling groups where veterans can talk and work with their peers to create their stories and experience the catharsis that the arts can provide while also telling their story to the public so that there is a better understanding of the challenges that veterans face.

Living my best life, for me, means that regardless of the circumstances you choose, you make the decision on how you respond to every situation. You can choose to respond negatively or you can choose to respond positively. You can also choose not to respond at all, although I wouldn't recommend that. Not facing the truth, your truth can cause you to find yourself in your own closet.

I think what I'm trying to say is that you decide what your best life is and not your circumstances, and not your problems. You have to be in charge of how you think about your situation or your circumstance because there are so many things in life and in this world, especially with the current political and social state of our Country that can really take you and keep you in a dark place if you allow it.

I thank God for bringing me out of the darkness because I know that I wouldn't be here without him. Remember, you also have a purpose, and whether you believe in God, or a higher power in the universe, or if you consider yourself spiritual, or none of those, there is a purpose for your life. The trick is to figure out what your purpose is.

I know that there are a bunch of anecdotes out there that people used to try to motivate you, but when you're in the dark sometimes that can push you even deeper. I think that most of us often believe that living our best LIE is living our best life. That's exactly what I thought too. Changing the way that you think it's probably one of the most important things that I can convey to you. Not giving up, not succumbing to the pressure, and continuing to push forward even when it's hard, because on the other side of hard, is life. Don't be afraid to step out of your comfort zone and live through the challenges, the rewards, and even some pitfalls of life. This is your truth and your authentic life. To leave this world better.

Action Steps

1. *Forgive yourself - Remember that no one can live your life, only you have that opportunity. To live your best life no matter what. Living your best life, because it is a constant opportunity to be great.*

2. *Trust yourself - Create a motto, to touch someone, and to spread love. This is as long as you're breathing, every day is a new opportunity to be the best you.*

3. *Move on - There aren't things that you can't do, just things that you haven't done yet. It's okay to make mistakes but don't live in them.*

Resources

Website: www.blanketoffreedom.org

Social Media: Facebook - LaShone Garth

Podcast: https://www.blogtalkradio.com/thebwo

MARIE S. PIARD
Life's Second Chance

Quote

Psalm 28: 7

"The LORD is my Strength and my Shield, my heart trusts in him, and I am helped."

Biography

Marie S. Piard, native-born of Port Au Prince, Haiti, mother of three children, and domestic violence survivor. After surviving a domestic violence marriage, Marie made the decision to create an exit plan to relocate her family and start fresh and build a new life. She decided to continue her education and obtain certifications as a licensed hair braider, life coach, and patient care technician, and 15 years of experience as an Ophthalmologist Technician.

In 2010, Marie was awarded a Habitat for Humanity Home for her and her family. She loves serving her community by giving back to the less fortunate. She has served as the Vice President of Habitat for Humanity CHODO, and Vice President of the Heart to Heart Coalition and actively mentors the youth at the Big Brother Big Sister Organization.

Marie's goal is to empower and impact domestic violence survivors and to establish her very own domestic violence outreach center. Marie enjoys spending time with her family, catering food for the community, braiding hair, creating silk floral arrangements, and designing custom jewelry.

The key to being happy is knowing you have the power to choose what to accept and what to let go of.

For more than fourteen years, I was married to my high school sweetheart. When we met, life was amazing. We had three wonderful children, two boys, and one girl. We were both go-getters with similar goals in raising our family. We built two businesses, a towing company and a car wash, both named after the initials of our children, JVA Towing Inc., and JVA Car Wash. I ran both, while also working at a hospital.

Life challenged me with trials and tribulations. During all fourteen years of this marriage, I was mentally, verbally, and physically abused. The nightmare started when I was 7.5 months pregnant with our first child. I made a simple request because I was craving sweets. I asked my husband for a bag of Skittles. "Skittles!" he said. And before I knew it, he had knocked me to the floor.

I was in denial that this had happened. I told myself "He won't do it again." But the abuse escalated. After my son was born, my husband was very loving but it only lasted a few weeks. Many days I considered leaving and running away. But I did not. I kept telling myself the lie, "I don't want my son to be raised without his father." And, so I stayed.

I told him I was going to leave him if he didn't stop. And, he replied "Go ahead and try. I will kill you if you ever try to leave me." My son would try to protect me, but he would get hurt, too. For many years we all suffered from the abuse of my husband. All my children were traumatized.

My daughter was born two years after my oldest son. Throughout this pregnancy, I was hospitalized for days after being abused. At one point I worried the baby would die in my womb.

I prayed and kept asking God to deliver us from evil.

I started to think about how I could escape with the kids without him knowing. But, the thinking never materialized into action. It was as though I was a zombie of inaction, fear, and terror. Still misguided by the hope that things would eventually change, I found myself pregnant with our third child. Make-up sex took me there. I was now pregnant with our third child and found myself distraught, ashamed, disgusted, and despondent.

The abuse cycle continued month after month, year after year. Then, I could have seen what my children were witnessing. They were also being abused. The four of us would cry ourselves to sleep, many nights. However, even when I was fed up and frustrated by the abuse, I did not change my mind to run away with the kids. I somehow continued to think that being with him was better than the children having no father.

In the summer of 2006, I woke up early, got dressed, and dressed my two youngest children. I took them to daycare and went to work at the hospital. The worst thing a mother could have done was leave a child with an abuser. But, I left my oldest son behind. I was terrified, but I believed God would protect him. I had faith.

When I got to work, I immediately called a shelter, located an hour away from home and my job. By 5:15 pm I clocked out, drove to the daycare center, and picked up my four-year-old daughter and 18-month-old son. The three of us drove to the shelter. When I arrived at the shelter, I sat down, took a deep breath, and said, "Thank you, God, for peace." I stayed in the shelter for two months.

In August 2006, my husband made my oldest son call me. He was crying over the phone and asking me to come back home. It broke my heart, but I should have known it was a trap, and yet, I fell for it.

When I arrived at the house and upon entering the driveway, there were loud sounds coming out of the house. Video game sounds, I thought. Once I entered the home, I immediately asked my son, why was the tv so loud. But my son was so happy to see us. He jumped into my arms and cried, and said, "Mom, thank you for coming, I missed you guys so much."

Then, my husband came into the room, looked at me, and said, "Thank you for taking the time to come and see us. We missed you so much, and I missed you." I looked at him but had no emotions left in me to respond. I told him I was done in a firm voice. I told him I would not stay in this marriage any longer.

My husband froze, and tears ran down his face. He asked me to go into the bedroom to talk using this despondent voice. He said, "Let the kids have their bonding time together since they haven't seen each other for a while." I responded. "We can talk here." But he insisted we talk in the bedroom. I was chilled, fearful, and upset for having gone into the bedroom with him. As we entered the bedroom, I opened the door and sat at the edge of the bed right by the door. He came and sat next to me and pleaded not to divorce him.

I immediately got up and moved towards the door, then he got up and moved closer to me and put his hands around my stomach pleading and begging for me not to follow through with the divorce. While his hands were moving slowly from my stomach to my shoulder and neck. I immediately told him "I have to go."

The last thing I heard was my husband shutting the bedroom door with his foot while he put me in a headlock and choked me. I immediately passed out on the floor. Next, I felt my husband grabbing my foot and dragging me onto the carpet. I felt him, lift me up and drop me on the bed. I then felt my feet and arm being tied. He got on top of me and began punching me in the face with a closed fist. All I felt was my face going left and right, while the blows were getting harder and harder. He lifted me off the bed and tried to make my unresponsive body sit on the bed, while I was still tied up. Then my sight started to slowly clear up. He grabbed a 9 mm gun and pointed it at my head and said, "I'm gonna kill all five of us today."

With the gun still aimed at my head he said, "If I can't have you, no other man will." While he was looking into my shut, black and blue eyes, he said, "I'm going to kill the three kids. Blow their brains out in front of you. Blow your brains out and kill me. No other man is going to take care of my family." I heard his voice but I couldn't make out his face, my face was destroyed by his fist. I had a broken nose and a shattered heart. After a few minutes, my vision was cleared. He picked me off the floor and put me on top of the bed, then I saw my face in the mirror. It was indescribable.

I heard a knock on the bedroom door, it was the kids. All three of them walked in with fear and came towards the bed looking at my face that was black and blue, broken and bruised. The kids asked, "Mom why are you tied up?" "What are you doing Dad?" Then they ran out of the bedroom crying and brokenhearted.

After the kids left the room, he untied me and removed the cable cord from my feet and the belt from my wrist. He immediately sat next to me with his head down holding the gun. Tears started to run down his face and he said, "I am so sorry, baby. Please forgive me."

Now he was vulnerable and was desperately begging me not to leave him. This all reaffirmed my thoughts on the changes I was making. I hugged him while he lowered the gun. That night we all slept in the house because if I ever thought of leaving or running out with the kids, he would have shot us. I stayed. The shelter that I left to put out a search for three missing persons.

In the morning, I got up and told my husband, I needed to get the kid's belongings at the shelter. I told him I was going to pick those things up and would then come back. While heading towards the door, both of my sons ran to the front door and said, "Mom I want to go with you."

My daughter stayed and looked at me with this fearful look on her face. She said, "Mom, I want

to stay with Dad." I was heartbroken and disappointed. I was planning on leaving and never looking back. But God had another plan for all of us, even my husband.

I took his truck. The boys had jumped in it already. I drove straight to the police station around the corner from our home. I explained everything to the detectives. I told them my daughter was still at the house along with the gun, cable cord, and belt. A detective took pictures and my statement.

The detective left for the house and then called me to come and pick up my daughter. When I got there my husband was already handcuffed in the back seat of the detective's car.

I then transferred all of the kids to my van and drove back to the shelter. As soon as I got there, I told one of the advocates, please get me out of here. Please find me another shelter. I'm willing to drive anywhere. But, I do not want to be traced to my new location." I donated my van along with the license plate. At this point, one of the advocates drove me and my children to a U-Haul lot. The advocate gave me $200 for gas and food. I drove 14 hours to a new shelter location.

Tears ran down my face for 14 hours straight because the God I serve gave me "A second chance at life." Even when I was Broken, Battered, Beaten, Shattered, Bruised, Hurt, HEARTBROKEN, and Dead. I came out victorious.

As I look back, I viewed myself as nameless. My husband might as well have called me his property."

Today, I proudly call myself Marie Piard. I can only be thankful for all the mistakes I've made and all the lessons I've learned from them. I learned the hard way I cannot always count on others to respect my feelings, even if I respect theirs. Being a good person doesn't guarantee others will be good people too. You only have control over yourself and how you choose to be as a person. As for others, you can only choose to "accept them or walk away."

The biggest lesson I learned is never a failure but always a lesson. As for others, they can keep apologizing over and over, but if their actions don't change, those apologies are meaningless.

Have you ever suffered from domestic violence?

The lesson I hope I can impart here is this: There is always a reason when you encounter obstacles. God sometimes utilizes you to help someone who will need you in the future.

"Breaking free from violence is not easy, but it is possible. Remember: You survived the abuse; you're going to survive the

recovery. Anyone who makes you less of a human being needs to go. Period."

You must realize walking away from something unhealthy is brave. If you stumble a little on your way out the door —so be it. Sometimes it seems scarier to leave than stay due to the unknown, but always trust what you know. Trust your instinct.

You need to remember: you can't help people who aren't willing to do what it takes. You cannot change your partner. This is one of the most difficult lessons to understand. It took me too many years of abuse to realize the only person I could change was me.

I've learned to get rid of distractions and move forward. This takes courage, dedication, and strength. It takes a long time to heal; the longer a person stays, the more profound the wounds and self-doubt.

Overcoming the stigma means loving yourself deeply and turning that love into advocacy. I have always believed in myself, no matter what I was going through. I am stronger now, and I feel a lot better about myself. I don't know how I did it, but I know it was with God's Grace.   God will turn a Mess into a Message, a Test into a Testimony, a Trial into a Triumph, and a Victim into Victory.

Action Steps

1.   Domestic violence took me to a very dark place, but one must believe in themselves. This is the first step. Once I realized I believed in myself, I could go forward. Seeing my children made this easier. They were the motivation factors. The bitterness within me faded because it was time to rise up and search for how to be ``free," Believing in myself meant I had to realize this was not dying; instead, I was being planted.

2.   It may come as a surprise, but in step two, one realizes these dark places are prerequisites for developing a destiny because failure is what helps us grow. Yes, obstacles and disappointments are discouraging, but it is these very setbacks that cause something else to come into one's life. It might be a new opportunity or a different way of doing something. But in step 2, one has to realize failure is a part of learning to grow.

3.   Going through failures and dark times is only temporary. One must understand failures and disappointments are not there to bury you. No one wants to go through adversity, betrayal, or opposition. But to go through these dark places allows the seeds of recovery to germinate. Being in an abusive marriage and seeing the pain in my children's eyes could have been the end of me. But, I learned to accept that going through those dark places was necessary. This helped me discover what my full potential could be. One cannot discover their strength until they've gone through the obstacles.

****121****

Resources

Marie Paird on LinkedIn.

YVONNE THOMAS
Mirror, mirror on the wall

Quote

"Death is as much a part of life, as life is."

Biography

Yvonne Thomas is originally from Lake Okeechobee Florida she has four beautiful daughters and seven grandchildren she moved to St. Petersburg Florida in 2004 she has been working in education for over 30 years she has worked with children from ages six weeks to 18 years of age Yvonne Thomas businesses jumped into a visit Inc.

Educate youth for a new vision. As God gave her this vision as she educates children and parents on how to be successful in life she is attending SPC college in St. Petersburg Florida to receive her AA degree in early childhood education her dream and goal is to keep educating you to be successful Yvonne Thomas is in the process of putting a book together when you look in the mirror you see yourself but once you look in there what do you really see in the mirror as you look in the mirror can you express and understand what you went through when you look in the mirror do you really see the pain and the hurt you've been through or is the Mirror you looking into had a pain that you can't see. Because sometimes when you look in the mirror what do you think you see?

One day when my brother and I were out shopping getting some items before we went fishing   one great memory, I remember is that when I would visit my brother every other weekend, and we would have cookouts together and we would always go fishing as my stepfather took us all the time, we will sit on the Fish Creek for hours and talk about the good times until we got a bite on the pole, I can say those was great memories for us to sit and talk about.

But most of the time my brother and I would talk about how we grew up in our grandmother's house and how we would always have to get up and go in the back of the house we had a farm back there where we had to clean the chickens and get eggs out the pin and we had to milk the cow as well then, we talk about. When my grandmother took us to the Orange Field with our grandmother one of the greatest members.

I can remember is when all of us is in our grandmother house, and we were all be sitting around and my brother he would start acting funny and do crazy things My brother was always the one that wanted to keep everyone laughing so when my brother and I got together we always talk about good times and talk about how we were raised up in the little country town Okeechobee Florida. The main thing that comes to my mind is that we were never able to go outside we could not go out the gate and play with friends we always had to stay in the gate or we couldn't be outside when the street lights come on because we knew what that means don't let the dark catch you there are so many memories that I can go on about me and my brother that can go back a lifetime.

I felt like my world was coming apart on this day the pain that I feel I was saying God, how do I get through this pain on September 6th, 2021, I lost my baby brother.

I had talked to my brother the night before we had even prayed on the phone, he said sis am going to be alright am coming home he said, sis I love you and I said I love you and then hung up the phone, the next day I got a phone call saying my brother had passed. It felt my world had ended; I kept saying lord why my brother. I kept praying and asking God to heal my brother it was like my heart was beating so fast, I said Lord what am I going to do with this pain, that I was feeling I've never felt this before.

When my grandmother and dad and stepfather died, I thought I felt the pain, but I can't understand this pain it was a hurting me so bad. I feel like I was falling to pieces inside as time passes, daily I learn to deal with my brother passing.

I would always smile on the outside, but I was hurting on the inside. When we go through the pain, we never understand how bad the pain is until we go through it. Sometimes the pain we feel is hard to deal with and we tend to block the pain that we fell on the inside what I have learned with the pain is that when we go through the pain it hurts so bad sometimes, we don't know what to do we sometimes learn how to deal with the pain that we can handle.

Therefore, we don't understand that we can barely accept the pain that you go through you have had so many disappointments like relationships and people letting you down and through all the pain I had to encourage myself even through this pain I was going to make it but I had to trust God through the pain I was processing I had to pray and ask God to guide me because I didn't understand the process that God took me through.

Sometimes when you look in the mirror you may not see the pain you've endured. But life can break you down so slowly, it can come like a thief in the night to the point where one day you're left asking yourself what caused the pain. By looking in the mirror you see the pain that is looking you in the eye, that is you actually you see in the mirror. The pain that you see in the mirror can bluer out life if you let it, does the pain really hurt or am I just reliving the over and over?

We don't have to understand pain to feel it. Yet pain that is not acknowledge can start to take over, and have you missing out on the people you love who are still alive and here. When you are looking in the mirror do you see the pain or is it just hiding.

I also learned that having a healthy relationship with my family members and children is to have open communication. That way it will help you to endure what you are going through because you never know who will be there to listen when the pain hits.

Not allowing my ability to see the pain make me forget that there are other wonderful things about me some days it wasn't always easy to see through my tears but what God gave him can be taken away no matter how painful the experience I realize that the reflection in a mirror can be twofold it will show me my scars but it also reveals my beauty. This beauty was my inner strength, which seemed to know what I didn't know at that very moment. That this pain had a purpose and as I understood this better and by, I could allow my tears to fall and still know that I was ok.

Being able to be a real-time reflection to my children was also a blessing that to this day has shown that the purpose was bigger than the pain I was feeling; I was able to allow the mirror to remind me that it starts with me. Changing how my family and I deal with things that are a part of life because although we will cry less when I remember my brother. We have to be encouraged still; the Bible says it this way in this life you will have trials in tribulations and even in those moments I can know two things One that what we consider painful has a purpose, and lessons attached to it as well and two what is my blow about right that even paying staring back at me I can count it all joy

You might not always see the light that is shining through your pain but when the tears fall it began to release it build you up to come out of the pain that you are feeling this is when we have to trust God and the purpose of the pain that is being released

Being willing to accept what is happening to them and what is in front of them sometimes we see things that we are not willing to accept then we build up a wall to cover the pain but when you look in the mirror and ask yourself what do you say through your pain that you are looking at are you seeing the process are the purpose. Therefore, what I learn through this is to talk to my family about death because when my brother died it hit me so hard that I was so lost.

So, what I would encourage is for families to meet and talk about these things because what I learned is death is not easy to tell when it hits home. So therefore, when you talk about looking in the mirror and do you see this pain in the mirror you should ask yourself if the pain, I am looking at in the mirror is the pain releasing.

My hope is that you will not only just use pain but every experience to be a heavenly reminder. That we are in this world but not of it and that even death is a part of life. I believe somewhere scripture says that we should celebrate when someone passes away. Celebrating a loved one gaining their wings does not mean that you won't miss and that they will not be moments upset but don't let the pain still away.

The moment you can remember them allow your memory's serve You with the gift of remembering the special moments you've shared together.

Actions Steps

1. *Develop a set prayer life. Make intentional time for yourself with others where you and God have a relationship. This will assure you that you are not alone because the presence of God has the power to make a dramatic difference. When you invite him into any ordeal life can dish out.*

2. *Get familiar with your Bible. Find scriptures that speak to you and write them down. This will provide you with a sense of security when or if emotions return. You will be able to carry these with you for confirmation that everything is ok.*

3. *Trusting the process. Removing your foot off the gas. Allowing yourself grace in your time of need. You will have moments where you need to know that it's perfectly fine to still cry and feel comforted at the same time. Don't be afraid of knowing it's ok to not have all the answers.*

Resources

FB Yvonne Thomas

yvonnethomas23@yahoo.com

BLAIR GREEN

From Indoctrination to Freedom

QUOTE

"Being yourself is the best thing you can do for the world because there is only one you and the most precious things on Earth are rare."
- Blair Green

Biography

Blair Green is a wife and mother of two, a Washington DC native, and a self-published author of the ultimate self-love workbook called the "All About You 30 Day Challenge a Workbook to Self-Love & Self Discovery Volume 1" Her mission is to help people find their superpowers and utilize them to create the life that they truly desire and live at their highest potential.

She is a Love Your Life Coach that specializes in unlearning your limiting beliefs and fears and replacing them with beliefs that are conducive to creating the life that you truly desire for yourself. She knows all is mental.

She believes if she can go from living in a strict Christian household that programmed her to not honor herself, to having to survive on her own while battling depression and anxiety, find the love of her life, reprograming herself for success, and thrive in a tropical country while creating the family life and *community that she always wanted then so can you? And she is willing and able to help support you on your journey to living the life you always wanted.*

It was a most eventful day. On my day of baptism, I was 10 years old at the convention in Richmond, there were thousands of people at the stadium. Around 20 people, including myself, were getting baptized that day, and I was the youngest. I had done a lot of studying the bible, learning scriptures, and remembering the answers to different questions and the moment was finally here. I was so proud of myself, and so were my family and friends.

After I was dipped into the pool, I thought I would feel different like I would feel more holy or connected with God but I didn't. I was just wet and excited about my life as a servant of God. Later, my family celebrated with me at the restaurant of my choice, and we had a wonderful time. After I was baptized, I was quickly held to a different standard. I was a sister of the congregation now, and I had to act the part.

If I did anything that could have been considered "worldly, " I was quickly reminded of my new position. With a line like "you can't do things like that now that you are baptized." Or "you're doing this, and you're a baptized sister?" paired with looks of disappointment or judgment. After hearing this about a dozen times, I quickly realized that my new position of being a baptized sister in the congregation was the new box I was put into heavy observation and judgment. Some people thought I wasn't ready to be baptized because I was so young and didn't fully understand the weight of what it meant to give myself to God in a Christian organization, and looking back on the situation, I agree. Even though I was smart enough to meet all the requirements on paper at such an early age doesn't mean I was mature enough to understand the weight of the situation.

I quickly discovered it felt like a short collar and a small box to fit into. As I grew up in the congregation, I learned how to deny myself of worldly pleasures and even lie to myself about what I wanted to be in alignment with what people in the congregation said was acceptable. This cut me off from my intuition, honoring my own desires and eventually even knowing what I wanted.

I was simply living for everyone's approval and what everyone told me was acceptable because I was a child, I trusted the adults in my life to lead me in the right direction in life. I tried my hardest to fit in and always be a good girl, but nobody explained that this would become increasingly more difficult as I went through puberty.

I kept being looked at as a mess up any time I did something that wasn't on code with what the congregation thought was best. This was embarrassing, emotionally exhausting, and all-around terrible for my self-esteem. I know pressure makes a diamond, but I felt like a crumbling rock underneath all the pressure from everyone in the community. It felt like they were all watching me, judging me, and just waiting for me to fall so they could speak on my demise. This wasn't healthy for my self-esteem or how I viewed me at all. I became very depressed and started to cut myself and inflict other pain on myself because I believed I was bad and needed to be punished. I knew this couldn't go on forever and needed a way out.

I remember the day I was done, the day I had decided that I no longer wanted to be a part of the cult that I had grown up in my entire life. I was in the 10th grade on a field trip to see a play. I don't remember the play's name or even what it was about, but I do remember the main character vividly. She was a beautiful, vibrant young lady who was a beacon for what it looked like to pursue your dreams in real life. She was just radiating positive energy and charisma.

As this young woman sang, danced, and acted out her part beautifully, she activated something within me that day, and I remember hearing a voice in my head saying that I will never be able to go after my dreams of living as a Jehovah's Witness. I know you probably thought I was a part of one of those 'living off the grid, with some narcissist man abusing his power type of cults' when you heard the word cult, but no.

I was a part of a Christian base, a very organized, actively recruiting type of cult. Most people are a part of cults and don't even know it, some are very different from the one I grew up in, but they are cults all the same. I know when I was in a cult, I never knew, and if someone at any time had the nerve to tell me that I was in a cult.

I would have been extremely offended and sent them to hell in my head. If you come from a Christian-based cult, I mean background, you probably know what that means. The word cult is the root word for culture. Every religious group, school, sorority, and fraternity has its own culture.

So, depending on what you're a part of, you're probably a member of a few cults, but I digress. After leaving the play, I had made up my mind that I no longer wanted to be a Jehovah's Witness, and I wanted to grow my hair in dreadlocks. That's all I knew for certain, and I felt very strongly about it. So, like a fool,

I told my two closest friends in the congregation what my plans were and of course, they quickly talked me out of it.

I had been baptized since the ripe old age of 10, and leaving the cult was basically social suicide. All my closest family and friends came from the cult since I wasn't allowed to spend time with outsiders like classmates, stay at after-school activities or even play with the neighborhood children was strictly forbidden. Any time I asked my dad why I couldn't stay after school for the school dance, he would quote the Bible at me and say, "Bad associations spoil useful habits." —1 CORINTHIANS 15:33.

If I were to leave being a Jehovah's Witness, I would be excommunicated from the community entirely. Everyone I knew and cared about was a Jehovah's Witness, and if I, the golden child, who decided to get baptized at 10 Years old, quit, all my friends and family would have been so disappointed and heartbroken.

I knew this before going to my friends, but something in me knew that I couldn't keep pretending, hiding, and lying about who I really was and how I really felt. I wanted the freedom to be whoever I wanted, even if I didn't know who that was yet. I just knew I wanted to do it on my terms without judgment or the guilt of letting others down. Judgment is a huge thing in the Christian culture, and it can crush you if you let it.

Fast forward 2 years later, I was disfellowshipped from the congregation and shortly thereafter removed from my comfortable 5-bedroom 4 bath home in the suburbs of Bowie to be put into a small 2-bedroom apartment in the hood of Oxon Hill, Md. For those who know, know this was a total shock to my system. To make it even better, I was ill-prepared to be on my own at the age of 18.

I had no money management skills, no direction, and absolutely no network to call on. My closest friends could no longer speak to me; their parents made sure of it; everyone I knew was treating me like a plague. After I was set up in my apartment, even my parents stopped talking to me. My dad stopped talking to me before that and dealing with this as a huge daddy's girl really broke my heart, but I really didn't have time to be sad about being isolated and stripped away from everyone I ever knew and loved because I had rent due.

Looking back, I'm forever grateful they didn't just put me out on the streets to figure it out on my own. My mother ensured I had a place to lay my head, which was a true blessing. Once I was all on my own, I thought to myself, "Finally, I am free to do what I want!" but little did I know that I still had the mindset that the cult had indoctrinated me with. I still shamed myself for my sexuality and held myself back from being my authentic self because I thought it was inappropriate or shameful. I still lied to please others and avoid confrontation. I still cared way too much about what others thought about me and judged myself harshly. I didn't know how to build bonds with people that weren't a part of my cult even though I was no longer a part of it anymore because I wasn't sure who was safe to be around.

My cult taught me to judge people's character by the way they served God and the position they held in the congregation. I didn't trust my own judgment and was completely blocked off from my intuition. I thought I was bad for not wanting to be a part of my cult anymore, so I punished myself by slaving away at dead-end jobs and, for years, not enjoying my life and wouldn't allow myself to have fun or experience new things. On top of all of that, being in survival mode didn't help. I was extremely depressed and used drinking to cope.

In 2014 I had my 1st child and needed support, but I didn't have anyone trustworthy to depend on. Years after that, I went through homelessness for about a year after losing my apartment. All these tribulations really shaped and changed me for the better without my knowledge. To bring you up to date with where I am now, I have completely reconditioned myself from the old cult way of thinking to a freedom mindset. From being full of shame, feeling depressed and anxious to experiencing peace of mind. From working 3 jobs and driving Uber to working from home as a stay-at-home wife and mother.

From being one check away from being homeless to being financially stable enough to pay my rent up for an entire year at a time. From emotional eating and being overweight to being in the best shape of my life and eating cleaner. Most importantly, I reconditioned my mindset to be at peace with myself, to love and accept myself, and my life started to blossom in ways I never imagined. "Be transformed by the renewing of your mind." Romans 12:2

1. Nothing starts before peace begins.

2. Question everything; if it does not make sense to you or resonates with your soul, question it until you get an answer you can explain to others and live with. If you can't do either, forget about it. Critical thinking is turned off with indoctrination.

3. Just because you are learning new things does not mean you are superior to the people who are a part of your old belief systems. You are just now more accountable than the next person.

4. If you do not brainwash yourself, the world will do it for you. You have to choose your thoughts, beliefs, emotions, and energy. If not you will take on the vibration of others who you grew up around and run their program. Which is fine if you want the type of life they have.

5. Nothing is happening to you. Everything is happening for you. Always look for the opportunity in the problem. I know you have been through a lot in your life already and I want to ensure you know you are not alone. We all have a story to tell, but something that is so beautiful about life is that you are the writer, director, and main character in your story. So what do you want your story to look like from this point on? If I told you, you can have whatever type of life you want. What would your life look like? Think about it. Guess this is completely possible. You can literally have whatever you want with the right mindset, tools, plan, and execution. You must believe in yourself and formulate a plan to get to where you want to go. Yes, some days will be harder than others, but you are more capable and powerful than you know. Tap into your superpowers and rise to the occasion. I know you can do it.

Action Steps

1. Assess where you are in all areas of your life. Where are you happy, and what could use some work? Spiritually, Physically, Emotionally, Mentally, Financially, Personal Life, Love Life, and Family Life. You can rate them on a scale from 1-10. A good question to ask yourself is; Am I completely satisfied in this area in my life and if not, why is that?

2. Once you have all these categories rated. Take each category you want to do better in and ask yourself what you believe about the subject. For example; If money is what you want to work on, ask yourself what beliefs do I have about money. Where did I learn how to handle money? What examples do I have that have the results that I want in this area?

3. Set a Goal for one area of your life at a time. If you try to change everything at once, it will overwhelm you, and you'll feel bogged down and get nowhere, believe me, I've done it before. So start with one area of your life at a time. Formulate a plan in that one area on how you can have the results you want and begin to execute immediately! If you need help creating your plan or suggestions on where to start, reach out to me and we can make it together.

Resources

Website; allaboutyouseason.com

Social Media FB; Blair Green (Bella B Da Goddess)

LYNNETTE HARDEN
Finding God Finding Me!

Quote

Proverbs 23:7 *"For as he thinks in his heart, so is he."*

Biograph

Lynnette Harden is a mother of two adult children. She is an Atlantean byway of Chicago, Illinois. A graduate of George Washington Carver High School. An attendant of Atlanta Metropolitan College for nursing with a second minor in nutrition. She has a 32-year career as a life coach. Her lifelong goal and mission are to inspire people to live healthy lives on purpose. Her goal is to become a Certified Peer Specialist. Her latest endeavor is to become an author, where she shares life experiences with others on how to live a full life despite physical challenges.

At the age of nine, I became aware of a power greater than myself. My grandmother used to gather up all willing participants for church every Sunday morning. I was too young to rebel. Eventually, I asked my grandmother, "How do you get saved?" She said, "Baby, you'll know when it happens." What a response. I felt disappointed in her response. That was her opportunity to plant the seed for my foundation. I was trying to establish my identity at the time. Being an only child, I spent a lot of time alone, wondering what the point of life was. I had no role models. Thank God for the extended family. My cousins were like brothers and sisters.

My mom dropped me off with my uncles and aunts while they were out partying. Every celebratory holiday, I found myself being kicked to the curb. Because My mom was a drinker, there were many disappointing times. Like when promises were not kept, she would promise to take me and my friend to an amusement park which would not happen. There was verbal abuse with her drinking and without her drinking. I was called stupid a lot, or my actions were dumb. That may appear small, but words hit hard, especially when they came from the one you loved the most. I have heard it enough that I began to believe in battle with it today. I am my own worst enemy.

1 Peter 5:8 NLT - Stay Alert! Watch out for your great enemy, the devil. He prowls around like a roaring lion, looking for someone to devour.

At this point in my life, I decided to become the master of my own destiny. I started to mimic good and bad characteristics that I saw in other people that I admired. This one girl in elementary school had the coolest trot. I took that trot as my own. I was bullied as a child, which was a challenging part of my journey, but my cousins always taught me not to cry and to fight for the right to be myself. Dancing was my escape, and I absolutely loved it. I felt free when I danced. My mom decided to put me in dancing school, which I loved, but my grades weren't the best. Dancing school was my mom's leverage to get better grades in school. I knew then I wanted to become a professional dancer. Who knew that dream would eventually be crushed?

At the age of 12, my mom's job transferred her to Houston, Texas. I was in the 8th grade at the time. What a culture shock! In Chicago, I lived among all black people. So, when I moved to Texas, I was unaware that I was going to be primarily white people. It seems as if the bullying never stopped. The kids would call me jangles because I would wear my keys on my belt loop, and it would make so much noise they could hear me coming.

After my mom finally got sober, I still spent much time alone. She would attend a lot of AA meetings. While alone, I enjoyed riding my bike to the black neighborhood, where I felt comfortable. On my way there, I was excited to see the cows, bulls, goats, etc. It was a lot different than what I was used to. I enjoyed Texas, but I missed Chicago. I lived in Texas for a couple of years. I knew by this point I felt comfortable enough to move in with my dad in Chicago. High school was much the same as elementary school, I was thought to be in a gang of my attire.

At the age of 16, I began to have run-ins with other girls. I remember my last fight. I was walking down the street going to the corner store. When the same girl would always talk about me as I walk to the bus stop for school. She decided one day too, accidentally on purpose, to kick me, and I snapped off and put her in a headlock, then proceeded to beat her in her face. Her girls jumped in it, but I had the best of her. She was the leader of the crew. I had no other issues with these girls. Pushing her in front of a car was an afterthought. I was so angry. By this time, I had grown into my own identity.

Jeremiah 1:5 KJV - Before I formed you in the womb, I knew you before you were born and appointed you as a prophet to the nations.

At the age of 17, I was a senior in high school. One night, I went to a blue light in the basement party and had my first drink. Not on purpose; it was in the punch. My boyfriend and I both passed out in the car; by the time we woke up, it was 2:00 o'clock in the morning. I tried to sneak into my house when my father flipped on the lights and proceeded to beat the hell out of me with no explanation from me. We had a tumultuous relationship. Later that year, I graduated from George Washington Carver, which was in the middle of the projects. I began college at 18, and my major was social work.

I thought with my history, of not liking people very much, I would not be successful at it. That was an afterthought. My dad thought since I was working at the Social Security Administration, he would charge me rent, although I slept in the same bed as my little sister. I didn't get very much support while going to school. He was the one who told me that taking the SAT would be a waste of time since he barely passed it himself. I would get up early to go to work downtown and then catch the bus to the other side of town to go to school. When I got home, it was 10:00 o'clock at night with a sink full of dishes waiting for me to wash after my family ate dinner. I didn't get the opportunity to study.

I moved to Atlanta, where I could get support from my mom. I did not get much support with my education from either of my parents. I did not know I had to be a six-month resident of Georgia to get my grants and loans. Therefore, I worked at

Piggly Wiggly during the day and at the IRS at night to make ends meet. My mom and I lived with my auntie, who was on drugs. My mom moved out then my cousin, and I moved out after she did. We got our own place. This was the turning point of my story. Before our move, I sought out a doctor about extreme pain in my shoulders. I was told that it was muscle strain from working at Piggly Wiggly. On the day of our move, I was fine getting everything loaded into the U-Haul and arriving at our new place. Once we got there, I took a break. I sat on the floor and could not get up.

My cousin thought I was faking and did not want to do the work. I was baffled. It only got worse from there. My whole body shut down. I couldn't walk. I couldn't clean myself. I couldn't open a jar, let alone open a milk carton. I couldn't comb my hair because I couldn't lift my arms. I found myself in a wheelchair with no diagnosis. I felt so helpless. Eventually, my mom took me to a specialist in rheumatoid arthritis and lupus. They took blood and diagnosed me with rheumatoid arthritis at the age of 19.

This was the first time I'd ever prayed. I was in a dark place. I smoked a lot of marijuana to cope. Ask me how I even rolled the joint; I do not know. Until they were able to find a medication that would relieve my symptoms, I was unable to work at Piggly Wiggly or the IRS. The IRS considered me A-wall because it was a seasonal position and I had to be there.

I leased an ice cream truck to pay my rent. That was the only job that was unsupervised. I told my cousin, who was still in disbelief, that she needed to find another roommate. I went to a support group for others suffering From RA juvenile patients. I only went to one support group. It was so depressing. I couldn't go to another one. It appeared that no one received any relief from the surgeries that they had. Atlanta had the most Ineffective rheumatologist, so I moved back to Chicago. I went to the Cook County Hospital. This is where I received some relief. The medication they put me on made me feel like a new person. Applied for Social Security twice in Atlanta and was denied twice. They wanted me to wait a year. I didn't have a year to wait. So, once I got to Chicago, I applied again, receiving it with back pay. My dream of dancing was over. I even had the opportunity to audition for Alex Haley and Company before my illness.

3rd Step Prayer:

Alcohol Anonymous 4th Edition

"God, I offer myself to Thee-to build with me and to do with me as Thou wilt. Relieve me of the bondage of self, that I may better do Thy will. Take away my difficulties, that victory over them may bear witness to those I would help with Thy Power, Thy Love, and Thy Way of life. May I do Thy always!"

At the age of 21, I stopped drinking and drugging. I start to go to church. I became an evangelist. I was celibate for three years before I had my kids at 24 years old. The relationship with my kids' father was some Jerry Springer show. I contemplated his murder, but he managed a recovery facility and never slept at home with me. That was God doing for me what I could not do for myself. I found out so much more about myself when I found God. And why I had to go through what I had to go through. God had to humble me for me to hear his voice. Now I understand why they say first seek the Kingdom of God, and all else will be given to you. Once my kids were potty trained, I got off Social Security. My doctors told me that if I worked a job, I would damage my joints. But I thought, how long would that take? I always believe that in life, you take chances and I wanted more for my kids.

I truly believe God would not bring me this far to drop me off. Spiritual life is not a theory. I've had my dark moments. There were times when I could not walk and dance. There were times when I had to recover from everyday simple activities. In my life, I've learned to find balance, physically, emotionally, and spiritually. It is so important for me to put my mind over matters. It is so important for me not to be around toxic people. I no longer must fight anything or anybody anymore. I can't let people have control over how I'm going to feel and/or respond. Today I respond, not react.

Matthew 4:19 NKJV - Then He said to them, "Follow Me, and I will make you a fisher of men."

I worked for Emory Healthcare for 15 years. I began having surgeries every summer. Neck fusion because I could not hold my head up. My doctor told me that if I was to be hit or fall, I would be paralyzed, or I could die from the blow to my head. It would break my neck. I had two knee replacements. After work one day, my knee locked up at the gas station and I could not move it. This is the first time my son has ever seen me cry. I had my second replacement the following summer. All of this was because of my arthritis progressing. My coworkers were not very understanding.

I found myself resentful. I couldn't talk to them. While I was struggling just to function, they were pissed because they could not take vacation time off. They even tried to get me fired by telling my supervisor that I fell out of my chair. Implying that I was high on drugs. I was drug tested and was found not guilty. I was enraged. It was not the first time I was enraged. My kid's father for not being there for my children when he told me he wanted kids enraged me.

So, I knew what that was. I found myself in the Employee Assistance Program office. I was having a breakdown. My job sent me to Ridgeview hospital for six weeks. While I was there, I suffered from panic attacks. I was diagnosed with stress, anxiety, and depression. I learned that I did not know how to deal with confrontation. I would stuff my feelings inside of myself. It made me sick, literally. Shortly after my six-week outpatient treatment, I resigned from Emory with all my benefits intact.

1 Peter 5:8 NLT - Stay Alert! Watch out for your great enemy, the devil. He prowls around like a roaring lion, looking for someone to devour.

Jeremiah 1:5 KJV - Know! Before you were formed in the womb He knew you, and you were born for such an appointed time.

Action Steps

1: Faith

Faith might waiver if what you are hoping for appears to not come to pass. Lack of faith was my dilemma until I searched for my innermost being. Thereby, I applied again, and I received it with back pay. My dream of dancing was over. I even had the opportunity to audition for Alex Haley and Company before my illness.

2: Servitude:

For years, I facilitated Inspirational meetings for the men and women in the custody of the Georgia Department of Corrections. I have mentored many women to live healthy lifestyles. I understand that no matter what happens to us in life, my mission is to testify that pain is inevitable, but suffering is optional. Serve others in season and out of season.

3: Purpose:

God allows things to happen to us. But to wait on God is rewarding. For, growth spiritually when we surrender to him. If I hold on to a situation so tight that my fingernail marks are on it, I have not surrendered. Today live your life with a purpose.

Poem: William Blake

"I sought my God and my God I couldn't find:

I sought my soul, and my soul eluded me.

I sought to serve my brother in his need, and I found all three.

My God, my soul and thee

Resources

FB: Lynnette Harden

Hardlynnette94@yahoo.com

TANISHA BORDEN
Peacing Me

Quote

"But the fruit of the Spirit is love, joy, peace, patience, kindness, goodness, faithfulness." Galatians 5:22

Biography

Tanisha Borden is a forty-seven-year-old woman; daughter of Cyril Borden and Arlene Jackson, born and raised in the city of New York. Her childhood dream was to become a nurse like her grandmother or become a teacher. She Is the proud mother of her son Jahshawn and grandmother to Hope, who has brought so much more love and hope into her life.

"T" as affectionately called by her family and friends; enjoys creating, photography, teamwork activities, and most of all helping others. After graduating high school, she joined the City Volunteer Corps, where she worked with team members delivering food to homebound residents, assisting teachers in public schools, and cleaning out junk-filled lots to create garden spaces for the youth.

With the help of her mother, Tanisha became a youth trainee for a New York City Housing Agency. She worked diligently for the housing agency after the death of her mother and rose up in the ranks quickly becoming a supervisor for 17 years. Her mission is to unite others by expressing creativity, community, and encouragement; she has found great joy in doing so. Ms. Borden invites you to be intentional in the ways you share and spread love.

I recall during the 80's watching movies cuddled up next to my mom eating an assortment of chips, pretzels, and popcorn in a brown paper bag (the original Party Mix). I will forever remember the times I spent at the park with my mother Arlene; I would love to stand on the swing while she would sit below and I would pump us up as high as I could. It felt so freeing as though we were flying high in the sky! I had not one care in the world; I just enjoyed being with her and feeling her love.

It was also very enjoyable when we spent time with friends and family. She was the life of the party! My mother would crack jokes and dance; her laugh was something else, it was a laugh that would bring a joyful smile to your face. No matter what pains and issues she went through, Ma was a very loving down to earth mother, friend, sister, and daughter. She battled with drug addiction for most of her life. We did not have much at all, which made me feel poor and less fortunate at times. The 13-inch black and white television with a hanger stuck into the hole where the antenna broke off and needing to use pliers to change the channels was one of the reminders, when I returned home from spending time at the homes of family members and friends. Regardless of not how I felt, Ma reminded me to be grateful, and patient and to always work hard.

When I was young, I always wished for my mom to live a drug-free life, nonetheless, she always handled her business, and was very open and honest She taught me about the wicked streets, traveling on the trains of NYC at a young age, the uncouth ways of some men, frenemies, sex, cooking, saving money, and taking care of my health. She always worked hard and did her best to provide and teach me what she knew. Ma respected herself and was highly respected and definitely took no shit! Her teachings were to ensure I was respectful and responsible. She was very tough on me, which I've grown to see was her way of guiding me to be my greatest self.

She was diagnosed with a life-altering illness in the late eighties. It was difficult at times to see her suffer; however, I am grateful we were able to spend more time together a couple of years prior to her ascension. Approximately two years prior to her moving on she stopped using drugs and made it her business to create joyful and loving memories I will forever cherish. We would laugh, joke, love one another and spend time with family.

I had been searching for a job for quite some time and in the spring of 1994, I received the great news of being accepted into a youth training program which was one of the last things my mother helped me gain to strengthen my life's foundation. My entry into the program made her so proud and I am forever thankful. I've always been dedicated to showcasing an exemplary work ethic, going above and beyond to ensure I learned the basics of several skill trades. I was amongst the top students selected to participate in boiler room technician training.

My mother never had the chance to see me graduate from the program because she passed away just a couple of months prior. I didn't have any family that lived in the same city, which made me feel alone. I was twenty years old, living in the apartment my mother and I once shared. Of course, family and friends called to check on me from time to time; however, people had their own lives to live. At the time I was making a stipend of less than $6,000 a year. I knew life had to continue on, so I focused on making money to keep a roof over my head and food *on the table. I had to request permission to go to my mother's funeral and was given four grievance days to figure things out.*

Ultimately, I put my dreams on hold, which meant not completing college, not adhering to my entrepreneurial endeavors, and remaining in New York City. My job kept me distracted from truly dealing with the loss of my mother. while the past memories were slowly resurfacing. Those pieces of me were popping up and spreading like a wild virus, which affected my peace.

I was able to conceal my pains and worries while working. I took my job very seriously, more serious than I took myself. I wanted to make sure I excelled at the job my mom helped me acquire so I can continue to make her proud. I chose to please my supervisors and residents. I was unhappy. I didn't enjoy cleaning up human feces, urine, graffiti, animal waste, blood, household garbage, and whatever else people managed to leave strewn about the corridors, stairwells, or objects thrown from the windows onto the housing grounds.

Working mandatory overtime twelve days straight every other weekend for many years resulted in me missing out on time with my son. If there were an inch or more of snow, I'd have to report to work at 7 a.m. working until 8 p.m. or later. That included fires, floods, blackouts, gas outages, and many other emergency situations. I was always there ready, willing, and able to do the work. I continued to keep quiet for the most part, allowing supervisors and others to take credit for my work, while many of them did much of nothing at all.

Even after reaching my goal of becoming a supervisor, not much changed except my responsibilities and dedication to my job. I was always the person everyone depended on and that practice was also a part of my regular life as well. I was the go-to person whenever someone needed or wanted something. It became difficult for me after a while because I didn't have many people to reach out to during my times of need. Although I never became a teacher or a nurse like I dreamed of career-wise, I was, in fact, a nurse, teacher, mother, counselor, motivator, and more to my staff, family, and friends

I filled many roles but I didn't realize how unhappy and broken I was. Not many people could sense when I was hurting emotionally, or physically or if I was in dire need. Expressing love, showing concern, and helping others when I was able to, all while keeping a smile on my face. Unfortunately, I would always forget to ensure I received and experienced the same love and dedication to myself.

Unexpectedly I was injured in 2020 and was no longer able to perform my duties. I no longer had my job to keep me distracted. I had the time to sit back, relax and reflect on my childhood. I realized I never took the time out to heal from the trauma I've endured.

I managed to bury much of it deep down inside of me for most of my life. It was as though I took a shovel and buried my traumas hiding those pieces of my being from myself as well as from others. Everyone has a story and I appreciate the opportunity to share mine with you.

It was extremely hard for me to do for a very long time due to feeling ashamed and fearful of what others would say or how they would think of me; I felt the need and desire to please others, and be loved, and accepted by them.

I was fairly quiet, sensitive, and shy as a little girl. I've seen, heard, and been through a lot; however, I did not speak often. I grew up in the era of not speaking unless you were being spoken to, causing me to remain in what was said to be "a child's place." If that instruction was ignored, I bet I would find out the hard way with a backhand across my lips, belt, or extension cord lashing through my skin. Even when I knew I was right I kept my mouth shut because many times the repercussions mentioned above would still apply.

Keeping my mouth shut was one of the worst things that became a normal part of my life for way too long. No one ever really knew the life I lived, the way I felt, or what I went through; I hid it way too well.

I have overcome many traumas in my lifetime; physical and verbal abuse, bullying, molestation, teen pregnancy, running away from home, and witnessing gun violence to name a few. I had to deal with family members speaking poorly about my mother's addiction and checking our cabinets to see if there was any food, things like that have an effect on a child.

I believed I wasn't deserving of great things and not loving myself enough to see the amazingly beautiful person I truly am.

During my revisit with my past, I was able to heal, I accepted all parts of me. By spending more time with myself, quieting my mind, and listening to my spirit I was able to heal from my place of hurt, no longer allowing myself to be taken advantage of. In this practice, I have overcome my childhood traumas, self-doubts, lack of self-love, and feeling of the need to be accepted by others. I grew to love, trust and put myself first. I clearly see the beauty in me, both inside and out. I was able to fully grieve my mom leaving her physical body and reconnect with her on a higher level as well.

I know now why some say the apple didn't fall far from the tree when comparing me to my ma. Regardless of my tough life, I've always been motivated to help others and love them. I continue to do so by giving back to the homeless, encouraging others, and most of all, my compassion for sharing love & motivating others to do the same. I also spend as much time as I can with my son, granddaughter, family, and friends, making as many loving, memorable moments as possible.

In January of 2022, my cousin Ebonita introduced me to a loving, motivating community Manifest University, where I was fortunate to meet some amazing like-minded individuals. One of those amazing people was Sierra Clark; I felt a connection to her when I heard her story. I immediately felt her genuine spirit of sharing and spreading love. She is a heart coach, bestselling author, and much more, who sprinkled some of her love upon me and gave me the opportunity to become a co-author and further affirmed; I'm a Superlative Woman!

I have recently found a passion for making heart-shaped magical love wands, which I plan to teach others to create. My vision is for them to be used around the world. To signify the unity of sharing and spreading love, reminding everyone they are love and greatness!

I am so proud of myself and grateful for the courage to unbury and deal with those old pieces of myself while reclaiming "ALL Pieces of My PeAce!"

Once you decide to claim your peace. It will be as if you put a huge stop sign up when it comes to catering to the needs of others, before taking care of yours first. You then can begin loving yourself, regardless of your physical or financial situation. Having control of your peace and love for yourself is far more important than any job, person, place, or thing. That lesson was one of the best feelings in the world for me. I feel happier and freer than I've been for what seems like a lifetime.

Remember! Never allow anyone to make you doubt yourself, take advantage of, or discourage you. Always put yourself first and pursue your dreams. You are powerful, amazing, and fully capable of discovering and maintaining the peace and love within you! Never forget to always love you! Show up for yourself and always do what's best for you. Also, be encouraged to share and spread some of that love that is deep within because the world truly needs more love to be spread by all!

Action steps

1. Find a quiet place. Set aside thirty minutes to an hour of your time to create on a daily basis. Choose something you are interested in or something you already love to do. Ex. create some jewelry, create a meal, a book, a drawing, a dance, a song, etc. Creativity is infinite. Use that creative time to clear your mind and enjoy the peace you've created for yourself and the amazing creations you'll come up with.

2. Start a self-love journal. Purchase a journal or decorate a notebook. Take ten minutes daily or weekly to write down the things you love about yourself, some of your accomplishments, and the things you are grateful for. You'll see how truly amazing you are. You'll also be pouring some love onto yourself at the same time

3. Enjoy a peaceful walk. Spend some 222time enjoying a walk in the park or to a place you've wanted to visit. You can clear your mind, reduce stress while enjoying nature, get out of the house for some fresh air, get some exercise, possibly see some new sites, you may even meet a few people if that's something you'd like.

Resources

tanishaborden@gmail.com

WANDA C. HAWKINS
Finding My Superpower

Quote:

"The whole problem with the world is that fools and fanatics are always so certain of themselves, and wise people so full of doubt."

Bertrand Russell

Biography

Wanda Hawkins is a Family Nurse Practitioner (FNPc), who was born in Chicago, Illinois, the 5th child of nine siblings, a widow whose partner supported her throughout her career. She attended Chamberlain College of Nursing, earning a Master of Science Degree in Nursing MSN (FNP) with a specialty in (Psychiatry) and is a member of the honorary nurse's society Sigma Theta Tau.

She spent many of her adult years in Atlanta, Georgia, where she worked as a registered nurse (RN), at the Trauma Care Center of Grady Health Care System in cardiology nurse care. She later branched into the specialty of psychiatric care. The specialty care netted her Travel Nurse Contractual assignments with John Hopkins hospital in Baltimore, Maryland, and George Washington hospital in Washington, DC. And many other projects throughout the United States.

She later attended True Way Seminary College, receiving a master's degree in Divinity (M.Div.). She is an ordained minister. She is a peacetime United States veteran.

The co-founder of Focus on Family Faith and Action (Foffia) a one-stop shop shelter facility for homeless women, children, and women who struggle with addictions. She has a passion for working with young women. She spearheads a mentorship model that provides one on one instructions on a build-back better pathway on how to become your best self with a relatively easy step-to-step model.

Today she has walked into new frontiers and has newly found a passion for writing. She is the co-founder of UltimatePrimeAuthor.com. A platform to introduce new authors to a holistic approach to healing from the inside out through writing. She also is an author, empowerment coach, speaker, and health and wellness practitioner. Her first of three books pre-launched last year (Poverty to Prosperity) are about how a simple mindset transition can transform one's defeats into that of abundance.

I was a peculiar student for as long as I can remember. I had a problem with reading and comprehension, so I was held back in the third grade. I attributed my poor comprehension to the assault I experienced during the formative years of my life. It caused me to shut down. I became very aloof.

Later testing revealed that I suffer from dyslexia. I was granted additional time for tests and major exams. The extended time allowed me to pass my registered nurses exam and family nurse exams and practicums. I passed both with flying colors. However, this was not the end. I was determined to do more. I asked the education director at the hospital where I worked if they would accept my coursework from a school that offered a registered nurse program with a concentration in mental health. To my surprise, they said yes.

I was excited because everyone had told me there wasn't any hope. I embraced the challenge and started working full-time toward my bachelor's degree in nursing. However, it did not come easy; I had to study every day after work for at least four hours. I also had to take numerous notes during class, which can be very difficult with dyslexia.

When I started the program, there were no accommodations for dyslexia. However, I knew what I needed to do to compensate. First, I had to speak with the teachers and explain my situation. During lectures, they would speak slowly, allowing me time to take notes at my own pace. When I took the exam, the teacher read aloud all my questions slowly and clearly.

I received a B in every class with dyslexic accommodations. The teachers were so impressed that they encouraged me to further my education to become a registered nurse. My dream is to become an advocate in the field of dyslexia by developing a support group for disabled nurses and educating others on how to adapt so they can overcome obstacles effectively.

I want to provide support to nursing schools that offer accommodation for students with dyslexia. I want to develop something that will be a model for the entire country.

I want my story to be an inspiration to anyone who has a dream but thinks they can't achieve it because of their disability. I want to thank everyone who has helped me get to where I am today from the teachers who reduced the speed of their lectures to the people who work at testing facilities to allow me extra time to *take exams and to my friends and family. But most of all, I want to thank God for seeing me through it all.*

I just want to say that if you have a disability, don't let it hold you back because God will see you through it all and help you achieve your dreams! Here are some quotes that motivated me to rise.

"I can't change the direction of the wind, but I can adjust my sails to always reach my destination."- Jimmy Dean

"It's not what you look at that matters, it's what you see." - Henry David Thoreau

"If you can't fly then run if you can't run then walk if you can't walk then crawl, but whatever you do you have to keep moving forward." Dr. Martin Luther King Jr.

When I think of the word success. I don't just think about what society deems successful. Success is being happy with who you are and where your life is right night. That means feeling good about the progress I've made, no matter what that progress is.

Right now, I am happy with where my life is, and it's because of all the experiences that have made me who I am today. I am pleased, and I honestly would not change a thing.

There will always be people who make you angry or drive you crazy because they don't understand your goals and determination to succeed. That's why I want to create awareness and acceptance for those who have a learning disability! I have learned from this that anyone can achieve anything they set their mind to. It takes a lot of hard work, determination, and perseverance.

It's essential to have a strong support group of family and friends that push you in the right direction. And finally, never let your disability stand in your dreams' way.

Never give up. I want to make others aware of the impact disabilities can have on people's lives.

You can do anything you put your mind to! My life is a proven testament. I have been told that I am successful despite my dyslexia, but I want to be remembered for being a role model and an inspiration.

Quotes from well-known celebrities:

"Don't let your disability hold you back because God will see you through it all."*- Marylyn de Savant.*

"There's no such thing as failures, just lessons. Every lesson is an opportunity to learn something new." *Dwayne Johnson (The Rock)*

"If there is a will there's a way."*- Marilyn dos Savant*

You can do anything you put your mind to. It is not the journey it is getting there that matters. *Wanda Williams*

There is no such thing as failure, just lessons. Every lesson is an opportunity to learn something new. Dyslexia was always considered in school to be a success and a loss at the same time. I was successful because I knew every lesson. And that was successful because it took me twice as long to learn anything than it did other people. But again, even though we succeed in our own ways, what do others see? Someone with special needs who have succeeded above their potential.

Dyslexia taught me that overcoming your condition does not matter as much as your attitude towards it and how hard you work. I failed because my condition held me back without knowing it. Then I succeeded when I was taught that I could achieve anything if I worked hard enough. If you have dyslexia or another learning disability, then the world is your oyster! There are many ways to succeed.

There is no such thing as failure, just lessons. Every lesson is an opportunity to learn something new. Dyslexia was always considered in school to be a success and a failure at the same time. I was successful because I learned in every lesson. And that was successful because it took me twice as long to learn anything than it did other people. But again, even though we succeed in our own ways, what do others see? Someone with special needs who have achieved above their potential.

Dyslexia taught me that overcoming your condition does not matter as much as your attitude towards it and how hard you work. I failed because my condition held me back without knowing it. Then I succeeded when I was taught that I could achieve anything if I worked hard enough. If you have dyslexia or another learning disability, then the world is your oyster! There are many ways to succeed.

We don't talk about the well-known geniuses of our time who rose above their dyslexia, Whoopi Goldberg, Richard Branson, Tome Cruise, Leonardo da Vinci, Walt Disney, Jim Carey, Albert Einstein, Steven Spielberg, Jennifer Aniston, Muhammad Ali, Danny Glover, and Henry Wrinklier. The well-known actors and scholars have accomplished worldwide fame, financial prosperity, and a place in history and society.

I succeeded because my teachers recognized that dyslexia were holding me back. And by finding out more about it, I learned how to grow despite the condition. Dyslexia taught me that people can still be successful no matter their hands. I am delighted, and I honestly would not change a thing. What makes someone succeed without any form of motivation? My success came from being able to succeed in my own way because of hard work. I don't have time to go over this, but if I had a choice while writing this chapter for a wider audience, what type of dyslexia story should be written, then here is my opinion.

Action Steps

1. **Think:** *Think of determination when you think of the word success. Own it to yourself, not just think about what society deems as successful. Be determined in your quest to succeed. Success can be as simple as being happy with who you are and where your life is right now. That means feeling good about the progress you have made no matter what.*

2. **Focus**: *Focus on work ethic. You can succeed without reading advanced books or solving advanced problems. Instead, it can come down to the basics. Something as basic as Creativity may prove to keep your morale high, thus by working hard on whatever you must do, regardless of whether it's pointless or not. Some succeeded by finding something they love doing, and others found success by working hard on something they are good at. I grew because I kept on striving to achieve, no matter how successful or successless my other attempts were. I succeeded despite having dyslexia by working hard on things I was good at.*

3. **Succeed** *Some might think that confidence depends on the person's motivation to succeed. Dyslexia taught me that the world is most successful when you combine learning with your success story. Success is a branch attached to confidence. If you have dyslexia, everyone will tell you what you're doing wrong, but you just say to yourself that success comes with succeeding.*

Resources

wanda@ultimateprimeauthor.com

Instagram@ author.coach

lnstagram@loveworthliving

www.ultimatebestself.com

OurSacredSafeplace: Dial-in 605-313-4144 access code: 1083944#

JANELLE C. FORD

Mirror A Legacy

Quote

"Tell the truth to yourself first, then to your children."

~Maya Angelo~

Biography

is the owner of Solidified Visions, LLC. An international bestselling author, certified professional life coach, and mental health advocate, she captures the attention of many with her unconventional but personable aura and thought-provoking inspiration on self-awareness and accountability.
From broken to bold!

Janelle shares with women worldwide how she gained the tools to beat her depression with what she calls the P.E.A.C.E blueprint, which can solidify as a foundation in your day-to-day life, and navigation to tap into your superpowers. This signature topic has landed her on several platforms, featured on the internet and blog radio, such as The Kim Jacobs Show, a protege of world-renowned motivational speaker Les Brown, CWR Talk Network, and Business Talk Radio out of New York, to name a few.

She is now living in her superpowers in one of her many talents as a background vocalist for two 3x consecutive NAACP Image Award Outstanding Jazz Album nominee Nathan Mitchell.

2021-2022 Albums include:

Nathan Mitchell Presents: Donny, Duke & Wonder

Nathan Mitchell: Love Languages.

We stand in the mirror and see our mother's and grandmother's resemblances and features, we know of them, and what we think of them. Today, many people reference the strength of the old school woman, the family matriarch; her perseverance, how she stood the test of time bearing the trials of life through her children, and how she stood by her man, her unwavering loyalty, and strength. Whether you were blessed to watch and experience her for yourself or were told stories about her, from my viewpoint, the stories hardly ever sound like that at the end of most days, she felt empowered. To

me, it sounds more like her bearing things than her brewing and cultivating something powerful.

One of my favorite cousins, Tosia, and I, were having a girl talk one day, and she was telling me about a conversation she once had with an elderly woman. Tosia went on to say how she acknowledged the woman's strength and the years of marriage she built with her husband, saying to her, "I want to be like you when I grow up"! Unexpectedly, the elderly woman responded, 'No honey, I wish I were more like your generation of women". That response was yet another confirmation of many deep conversations that the women around me and I often have about the old-school woman. I don't think the elderly woman's response was valuable enough for us to feel we were right. Still, it was the confirmation that we are not wrong to believe that the strength and discipline that we possess and the dreams we desire for ourselves are valid, warranted, and admirable with the audacity to even believe so.

If you haven't already, imagine having a heart-to-heart with your grandmother or your mother about who she truly is, how she truly feels about life, herself, and the things that she desires. Imagine the power behind it. It would take years before my grandmother, and I began having heart-to-heart conversations. The generational gap is so widened even still today; I think some parents, especially old school parents and guardians, only have a few things they deem relevant when it comes to parenting; monitoring the child's behavior, feeding, clothing you, making sure you attend school and keeping you safe...missing the importance of the relationship aspect of it.

If you grew up regularly attending church, I think most would agree that in every church, there are the same few kids that were always there running around. Even if only board and committee meetings were on the agenda, I was one of those kids, bored, lying in the pews, talking to myself, and using my imagination to pass the time. Before we left home, I would sneak and call my aunt who lived down the street, ask if I could come to her house, then beg her to call our landline and mention to my grandmother that I could come over while she went where she needed to go.

With no hesitation, my granny would say, no! Janelle is going to this church with me. In church services, If I were caught playing or talking too much, she would pinch and hold my skin, walking me up the aisle through the double doors to the restroom to discipline me. My best friend and I of 37 years laugh until this day about how we had to be out of the house by 9 pm, to attend the teen dance at the recreation center, only having a solid one hour and a half to party, because we had to be home by 11 pm. Everyone knows that the party doesn't start jumping until eleven o'clock, so you can imagine how unfair life feels to me at this age and time...

My grandmother was the typical stern woman with strict rules, giving me minimal leeway and room to get into trouble. Not knowing then how to Identify what I know now. But the consistency in what she was adamant about in my day-to-day, yes! Some days felt unfair, but as a young girl with low esteem, there was something about it that I felt safe and secure.

I always reflect, thanking God for the heart, mind, and spirit that he blessed me with because many kids would develop hate or resentment towards parents with a stern tone, rules, and restrictions, but not me. I believe in my heart that it wasn't meant for my parents to raise me; based on who they were 44 years ago when I was born, they wouldn't have been able to raise me to be the brave and bold individual I am today. Nevertheless, God allowed my parents to be here today, clean, sober, mentally, and emotionally healthy and loving.

So, For me, it's right on time! I was 15 years old when I begged to move back with my mom after living with my grandmother since I was seven years old. My grandmother found every reason to stall because I'm sure at that point I was her life, her something more to live for. My aunt Joyce (RIH), my grandmother's baby sister, convinced my grandmother to let me go, and right in the middle of the school year, I moved with my mom. After being gone with my mom for close to one year, I wanted to move back with my grandmother, who welcomed me with open arms. Not long after moving back, I had to get up the nerve to tell her that I needed to start adult education classes to obtain my G.E.D because I was short of the required credits to graduate high school with my class. I know she had to understand and accept that reality was tough for her, but I think it was a pivotal point for my grandmother, and the generational gap between her and I began to close.

My grandmother unconsciously showed me the significance of being attentive to my children and their mental health. My oldest son, who is now 23, was in kindergarten at the time. I was frustrated, having a fussy morning with my children, and I remember, as if it were yesterday, my grandmother saying, " Don't ever send your children off to school like that!" It made me realize that no matter what I was dealing with, it was important to establish positive mornings and a peaceful home and lifestyle for my children and I.

You hear and read different definitions and perspectives of a legacy, it's been defined as inheritance, heritage, history, birthright, provision, and so on; however, I believe the foundation of legacy is when a family creates security, healthy life tools, love, laughter, respect, and their heart is safe with one another. Those attributes alone can give any family the power to cultivate unlimited aspects and a definition of their own to build a foundation upon. My grandmother planted so many meaningful seeds that when I look in the mirror, I see the value of improvisation, acceptance, giving, devotion, audacity, honor, solitude, and substance.

As a young divorcee and mom, there were many times when my money didn't add up to buy enough food and clothing for my children. Not that I couldn't have gone to my grandma for help because I very well could have, but because I spent Saturday mornings as a child with my grandmother and great aunt going to estate sales, rummage sales (as grandma would call them), thrift shopping, and the local pantry, those experiences became resources that helped me provide the necessities needed for my children.

It is true when they say, "If there's a will, there is a way." As a young girl, I never went without, and it may not have been the latest gadget or fashion, but it was what counted the most where I still felt cared for and safe.

I remember having a conversation with my oldest son, and he reminisced about one point in our life when I couldn't afford cable, and we watched DVDs and four good channels with an antenna that I bought from Big Lots. The antenna sat in the window nearest the television. With every channel we wanted to watch, we had to move the antenna at a different angle and tape it to hold it steady to get a clear picture. But my God! We were so content and at ease; my children felt safe and cared for.

Acceptance is a form of peace. And that is what we all witnessed for about ten years as diabetes slowly caused my grandmother's physical ailments and sickness. But have you ever witnessed a double amputee with more enthusiasm for life after their legs were gone?

Well, that was my granny, finding peace with her circumstance, going on every family vacation, to church every Sunday, cooking, and playing candy crush on her tablet in-between times. Countless times, in and out of the hospital, and rehabilitation centers, and being on a ventilation machine and a tracheostomy a couple of times, her faith never wavered. I went to visit her in the hospital one day; she couldn't talk because she had a tracheostomy for the second time. Still, before I could step in the door of her room, I noticed my grandmother looking up and using her hands as an expression; without any interruption, I stood and waited outside the door because I knew she was talking with God.

The Lord is Elnora's shepherd; Elnora shall not want. He maketh Elnora lie down in green pastures: he leadeth Elnora beside the still waters. He restoreth Elnora's soul: he leadeth Elnora in the paths of righteousness for his name's sake.

Even though Elnora walks through the valley of the shadow of death, Elnora will fear no evil: for thou art with Elnora; thy rod and thy staff they comfort Elnora. Thou preparest a table before Elnora in the presence of her enemies: thou anoints Elnora's head with oil; Elnora's cup runneth over. Surely goodness and mercy shall follow Elnora all the days of her life: and Elnora will dwell in the house of the Lord forever.

This is how my grandmother often instructed us as family and friends to circle her, touch and agree, and resight Psalms 23 in unison. She taught us to include Psalms 23 in our prayer life, our names, and others. She was brave and inspirational even at her lowest and weakest moments.

Our church pastor said it best at her homegoing service, "Elnora taught us how to suffer". She fought long and hard, praising her Lord and Savior, Jesus Christ, living a life that showed her loved ones a true example of faith and strength. Although she nurtured and raised me, she never allowed me to call her mother. But a mother's love is what she was. She is gone in the physical form, but everything about her is forever embedded within me.

She lived with a lot of physical pain, but I know her heart was happy because not only was she surrounded by love, but she was also able to see her only child and son live a clean and sober life as a well-rounded man. As well as watching the granddaughter that she raised to grow up to be a great woman and mother.

She lived to see the fruits of her labor bloom and not be in vain. In her own words: "GOD HAS BEEN GOOD TO ME!!" Amen. Ms. Elnora! Indeed, he has... We got it from here. We love you, and continue to sleep well!

It has been five years since she passed away. Today I smile more than I cry at the thought of my grandmother because she left me with such a foundation to cherish, implement and build on. She is I, and I am she She is Elnora B. Keith. My paternal grandmother, a super superlative woman, a legacy I am honored to mirror.

Words of encouragement:
When you heal yourself, you help heal your ancestors, your daughters, and family too. With all that you want to experience with your family, you have helped create it. So, be the love, understanding, support, and change you wish to see in your family. Love without keeping score.

Action Steps

1. Seek wisdom. Realize that there are levels to everything. Life allows almost everything you experience to teach you more meaningful than dreadful lessons. Henceas seasons change and come back around again, so should we gain mentally, emotionally, and spiritually.

2. Heal on purpose. What we present won't fix in us what's broken. Be intentional in identifying your generational curses, traumas, and limiting beliefs. Interview and find a personable and quality therapist and unpack. We can't rewind time or erase experiences, but with intention, we can build something with it.

3. Tap In. You were created to know the goddess within you; it's your birthright to learn and grow the tools within to build and sustain her. God will allow you to go through the same test until you learn the necessary lesson, so when you feel it's easier to remain the same, remember that everything attached to your peace, power, and fulfillment is on the other side of going all the way.

Resources

Instagram @iamjanelleford

Https://www.iamjanelleford.com

CORA SMITH

My Life's Journey

Quote

"It Is Not the Journey It's getting there that matters."

Biography

Cora Smith with Caribbean heritage. I am originally from Chicago, Ill. The mother of 6 adult children, seven grandchildren, and two great-grandchildren. A retired head chef from Chicago State University. I love arts and crafts, cooking, and spending time with loved ones.

A mother's love is eternal. It knows no bounds and can never be truly measured. It is the very definition of unconditional love. A mother's love is selfless, always putting her children's needs before hers. She is their protector, their confidante, and their cheerleader. A mother's love is solid and powerful. It can weather any storm and overcome any obstacle. Nothing can break a mother's love.

A mother's love is pure and true. It is the most honest and steadfast kind of love there is. A mother will always be there for her children, no matter what. Her love is never-ending, and she will always be there to support them, no matter what happens in life.

A mother's love is the most notable and unique kind of love in the world. It is a love that can never be replaced or duplicated. It is a love that lasts forever.

Even though I love the job of being a loving mom and grandmother, growing into the role of mother and grandmother was a time in the making after losing my mom at the young age of 12. I was thrust into the role of being a mother to my seven brothers and sisters. Then at the age of 15, I became a mother to my first child.

Although I was scared and didn't know what I was doing, I knew I had to be vital to my child. I had to be the one to show them the way and help them through life's challenges. I had no choice but to step up and be the best mother I could be.

And so, even though it wasn't easy, I became a teenage mom in the making. And over time, I learned how to love and care for my children unconditionally. It took the death of my only daughter to bring this out in me. Before her untimely demise at 21, she was a teen mother herself. I became a mom at the early age of 15. Life was hard but being a teen mom was harder.

There are so many things you want to do and be in life, but I had to put your child first. I can say from experience that it is worth it. Although my daughter is no longer with me here on earth, she has left me with my grandchildren with the most precious gifts imaginable. Through them, her love and presence still shine brightly in my life every day.

Being a mother, grandmother, and great-grandmother who has experienced the ups and downs of motherhood firsthand. I know the challenges that mothers face, but I also know the immense love and joy that comes from being a parent. It is the best feeling in the world to see your children grow up and have their own children.

I raised my children in the home of an emotionally unavailable and possessive husband. It was not an easy task to keep my children shielded from his outbursts or the hurtful things he would say during arguments.

I had to be extra careful about what I said in front of them and often had to explain his behavior away from work stress. I constantly walked on eggshells, never knowing when he would lash out.

When I was being abused, I was too ashamed to let anyone know when I was being used because I feared their judgment. I was embarrassed that I had made such a poor choice and worried that I would be judged for not leaving him. See, I thought it was only me. That's what shame is. The word Shame is believed to be derived from an older word meaning "to cover," as such, covering one's self, literally or figuratively.

What I came to learn is that I wasn't doing a very good job of hiding it. People could see that I had lost my spark and my heart had been broken. My once sassy, independent, confident, capable spirit was long gone.

then the day came when the pain of staying was worse than the pain of leaving. So, I packed up all my troubles and left with all of my children. That moment, that freeing moment...was a fabulous feeling of liberation from the abusive oppression I had become accustomed to. Although I feared financial insecurity and the magnificent task of a complete makeover of my entire life, I did learn that I was not alone. In fact, 1 in every four families experiences domestic abuse. Statistics are great, but I prefer visuals. If I was in a room with a dozen people, three of them have been where I have been or are currently where I was.

Those same statistics show that there is no cultural or economic divide. It doesn't matter if you are rich or poor; it is still 1 in 4 families. But either way, you can leave. It's alright. Being abused is never ever your fault. I have found it to be an incredible life-changing, life-growing experience to share my hope and strength and BRAVERY in setting myself free.

It was challenging to keep my children safe and protect their innocence in such a toxic environment. I often felt like I was failing as a mother because I couldn't give them the stable, loving home they deserved. But I did the best I could under the circumstances, and I am proud of how my children have turned out. They are kind, compassionate, and strong individuals who have been through a lot in their young lives. You are doing amazing.

If you are raising your children in a home with an abusive husband, know that you are not alone. It is a complex and challenging task, but you are doing a fantastic job. Your children are lucky to have you as their mother. You are strong, you are brave, and you are doing an amazing job. Keep going. Your children need you.

This is a complex and challenging task, but you are doing an amazing job. Your children are lucky to have you as their mother. You are strong, you are brave, and you are doing an amazing job. Keep going; your children need you.

Keeping your children safe and protected in a home with an abusive husband can be challenging. You may often feel like you are failing as a mother because you can't give them the stable, loving home they deserve. But it is important to remember that you are doing the best you can under the circumstances. Do not get lost in the cradle of Shame.

Planning for safety - If you have time to plan, start putting aside cash again, preferably somewhere other than your house. Leave some clothes and important items with a friend in case you have to leave your house quickly. And start documenting every incident of physical or emotional abuse in your household, whether it involves you or your kids. Make a note of the date and time the incident occurred, and exactly what happened. Also Make a list of safe people to contact memorize phone numbers of people or places you could call for help keep the change (for a pay phone, as you may find yourself without a cell phone) with you at all times, as well as cash for living expenses, and establish a code word with family, friends, and coworkers so that you can tell them to call for help without alerting the abuser. You should also prepare to take important papers with you, such as your credit cards, checkbook, social security card, birth certificates copies of deeds, leases, insurance policies utility bills (for proof of residence) proof of income for you and the abusive spouse or partner, such as pay stubs or copies of W-2 forms, copies of bank or credit card statements if you cannot easily access them online, and any documentation that proves past abuse, including photographs, police reports, or medical records. If You Have to

Leave quickly - If you have to leave your home quickly to escape an abusive relationship, go to court immediately for protection that requires the abuser to stay away from you. If you have children, be sure the order gives you custody. Otherwise, you may be accused of kidnapping. If you have the resources, it's wise to hire a lawyer at this point. But don't worry if you can't afford to pay for legal assistance; many resources are available to help you. If you go to a shelter, the staff should be able to help you find legal aid quickly to file the necessary papers.

Many courts have domestic violence resources, including restraining order packets with instructions, clinics with clerks who can help you with the paperwork, or judges who are available to sign restraining orders and custody orders on very short notice. You have access to the court 24 hours a day in some places.

Usually, you also will be able to quickly find help with delivering legal documents to your spouse; the local sheriff's office is generally charged with this task. You have to get the papers delivered (served) before they take effect.

Whether you had time to plan or had to leave in a hurry, there are steps you can take to stay safe once you're away from the abuser. Immediately change your phone number and don't answer the phone unless you know who is calling. Be sure that your new phone number is unlisted and blocked so that it can't be *easily discovered. You may also want to rent a post office box or arrange to have your mail delivered to the address of a friend or family member.*

Action Steps

1. Safety Planning

Get yourself and your kids to safety. Statistics show that the most dangerous time for women living with batterers is the point at which they leave the relationship. The vast majority of battered spouses or partners are women, but if you are a battered man, all of this advice applies to you as well.

This means that you will need to find housing somewhere that the abuser can't find such as a battered women's shelter, a hotel, or the home of a friend that the abuser doesn't know. Don't go to your parent's house, your best friend's house, or somewhere else where the abuser is likely to look for you

2. After You leave

Whether you had time to plan or had to leave in a hurry, there are steps you can take to stay safe once you're away from the abuser. Immediately change your phone number and don't answer the phone unless you know who is calling. Be sure that your new phone number is unlisted and blocked so that it can't be easily discovered.

3. If the abuser does contact you, make a note of when, how, and what happened.

4. If you are staying in your home, change the locks

5. don't stay alone

6. Change your routine frequently

7. Think about how you'll get away if the abuser confronts you

8. If you have to meet the abuser, do so in a very public place

9. Contact people you trust at your workplace and your children's school so they can be alert for anything unusual.

10. Legal Protection

11. Many courts have domestic violence resources, including restraining order packets with instructions, clinics with clerks who can help you with the paperwork, or judges who are available to sign restraining orders and custody orders on very short notice. In some places, you have access to the court 24 hours a day.

Usually, you also will be able to quickly find help with delivering legal documents to your spouse; the local sheriff's office is usually charged with this task. You have to get the papers delivered (served) before they take effect.

Resources

FB: Cora Smith

cgladstone69@aol.com

FLOWER YISREAL
The Scraps of Life

Quote

"To sew is human…to produce is noble."

Biography

Flower Yisreal has lived in Okinawa Japan, Philadelphia PA, and Harlem, NY, however, she claims Hampton, Virginia, as her hometown. Flower is a state national of California. She studied photography, film, and anthropology before completing her Computer Science studies at Temple University.

Her writing style is a flowing mix of data analytics, non-fiction parables, poetry, proverbs, and scripts. Her first published writing is a song; her second was a patent for the braided fabric crown, and her third child, Flower Torah, inspired her third. She published "Just Like Me" with her full-of-light 4-year-old, Flower Torah, with a message to young new readers; to bloom in all seasons.

She spends her days playfully and purposefully homeschooling her children, designing her art & garbs, and creating honest dialogue that empowers her community to accept responsibility. She is a supportive daughter and sister, a loving mother of all children connected to her, and considers herself a powerful creator. Flower currently resides in her hometown.

I had a corporate IT job, a good salary, health benefits, and a 401K package. I had Sundays to spend with my family. One day I got the nerve to quit cold turkey. I then started my first company, an IT consulting firm. Initially, I wasn't generating any income and had to leave Philadelphia to move back to my hometown.

Everyone in my family was bewildered that I had left my good job. After some months flew by, it became obvious that I needed to find an additional income. I accepted a part-time job at a department store. While working at Nordstrom, I immediately found myself dreading my work environment. One day, in particular, became the day that changed my pursuit of happiness.

I was helping a gentleman customize his suit. A seamstress from the tailoring department came to assist me. While she was there, I began asking her loads of questions. I followed her back to her department to watch her customize the gentleman's suit.

I noticed boxes of fabric under her sewing station. I inquired about the fabric, and she informed me those scraps from the altered clothing were thrown away after each work day. Instantly, a light bulb illuminated my spirit. I asked her if taking the scraps home with me would be okay. She casually answered yes and looked at me with questioning eyes.

I rushed home that night with bags of fabric scraps and began brainstorming ideas of what I could make with them. I had no idea why I wanted those scraps, but in hindsight, I learned how important it is to trust my intuition. At the same time, I was dating a man who wore scarves around his head. I would watch him wrap his head with scarves and I would roll my eyes at how long it would take him. I decided to design a solution for that.

Night after night, I would sit on the floor in my childhood room at my parent's home, designing what I eventually described as a "crown." I hand-stitched pieces of fabric together and began making the first one. Once I was finished with the first crown, I placed it on my eldest son's head and asked him how he felt. At the time, he was writing an essay about the black panther, Assata Skahur, and he said he loved the crown because it made him feel powerful. It was the confirmation I needed to hear.

I quit my part-time job a week after I designed my first crown. I began creating another crown, and this one came out even better. I offered this crown as a gift to the man I was dating. As soon as he placed it on his head, he said to me, "we should sell this," and so we did. About a month later, we published an online store. We sold it everywhere and grew our sales fast.

A few months later, even though my gut told me this was hasty, we decided to commit to each other and soon thereafter we birthed a child. Our love story was real. Our new business was real and extremely successful, it began to trend. Everything seemed to be happening at lightning speed.

My crowned King was the head of our family. I followed his lead on everything, as I thought a righteously submitted wife should. However, any ideas I had for our family and business were tossed away like scraps of fabric after each workday.

Quickly our life began to take a sharp left turn. From the outside looking in, we were a flourishing power couple focused on our legacy. Yet behind closed doors, we were consistently physically, emotionally, and spiritually scrapped. I worked from home, making crowns night and day. I served my family, community and I did so purposefully. However, I kept feeling this anguish in my gut that something wasn't right. We didn't always have a place to call our home. That was my biggest worry. I worked in hotel rooms and on friends' kitchen tables. I slept on floors and lived in the projects.

It was beyond the humble beginning. The struggle in my life and marriage was surreal. I had even less time for my children. I worked on the crowns, worked harder as a parent and worked my hardest at having a harmonious relationship. Nothing seemed to work. The harder I tried, the worse it seemed to get. We broke up several times in a four-year timeframe.

I kept a lot bottled in. One day after a heated argument that turned physical, I left him and moved back to Philadelphia. There I was pregnant and without any means of income. The only thing I had was this creative desire to continue designing. I wanted to start selling the crowns again but my husband had dissolved our business and locked me out of all business accounts. He told me that the business was his and that I wouldn't be successful even if I tried. His words left me speechless and I agreed with his perspective that I would be nothing without him.

"I'd be a baby momma with all these baby daddies," he'd say to me. For a while, I agreed with his voice as it played in my head. My voice was null and void, and all I could hear was fear. Fearful and broke; I could not afford to just wallow in my misery. The children deserved more and were hurting too. Even though it didn't feel that way, this was the best thing for me at the time. It offered me the lessons I needed to learn. I had to let go of the blame and start to regain the courage to decide who I wanted to be and what I wanted to experience.

I could see the scraps of my courage that I buried underneath the pain of my decisions. Determined to make a way, I used what I like to call my simple life hack. It helped me begin designing and re-aligning with what I had buried six feet deep. I decided to simply empower others. That was it. I needed someone to uplift me and so it just made sense for me to give what I wanted to gain.

Even though I was growing through an uncomfortable transition, I decided to start with this heart-worthy mission. I had to start from scratch but was motivated to serve. I began to create again, and this time without any scraps. This time, I had to turn nothing into something.

I had to lead myself into the light of living and release what was no longer serving me. I focused on what brought me joy, and that was my creativity. I began building my new business. The verbal abuse, the emotional trauma, the domestic violence, and the distilled fear in the air lingered heavily in my spirit. I'd have day-mares of the tragic scenes repeatedly playing in my head.

I was still very much attached to the trauma of the past. The business started slow and I began doubting myself. I was in my last trimester with our second child and it started to get very scary. Doubt ran an unnecessary muck in my head, fear challenged my creativity, and my addiction to them both sent me running back to him. Fear led to my desire to bring my family back together and find our way back to what had the potential to be true love. When I came back, he was happy. We were happy. Until we weren't.

I allowed him to lead us down the same path yet again. I worked nonstop. I managed our two babies and now his new business and the business I created for the crowns. I worked even harder than before. I kept the trauma playing in my head and quietly played along as the loving, surrendering, apologetic, and submissive Queen I was cast to play. That was my role. He was my Lord, but he saved me not.

The voice in my head raged in curse words sharper than the truth I dared not to utter. We were still scraping behind closed doors. His loud and thunderous voice was consistent with my bottled-up sugar-coated silence. One night he reserved a hotel room so we could spend some time together. That night, I fell asleep with an unsettled spirit.

INT. NIGHT. CHEAP HOTEL ROOM. NO LIGHTS ARE ON. THERE IS LIGHT COMING IN FROM OUTSIDE THE WINDOW.

A woman lying asleep in the bed. A man standing near the cracked window. Through the hole in the window screen, he ashes his smoking cigar while staring at a cell phone held in his other hand. The light from the phone illuminates his face. His facial expression looks disturbed.

The woman wakes up and rolls over to see the man standing and now staring at her with tear-filled eyes.

MAN:

You fucking bitch, you lying ass stupid whore!

WOMAN

(She sits up in the bed)

Is that my phone?

MAN

(Shaking his head, no voice trembles)

You are so disrespectful man!

So that's how you think of me, huh? You think I'm some

Lame-ass simp ass n*gga, huh?

The woman begins to get out of bed. She walks to the dresser near the table, placed a foot away from where he stood. She picks up some clothing and gets dressed.

MAN

(With smoke coming out of his mouth)

Oh, you're just going to ignore me and leave, right? That's what you always do.

Fucking got nothing to say to me about the fuck shit you be doing behind my back, but your fat ass can text your girlfriends a whole fucking essay. Talking about how my ass isn't providing for my kids.

The man begins walking closer to the woman as she gets dressed. He gets close to her face with the phone.

MAN

(His voice escalates)

Just lying about how I'm talking to all these hoes out here and how I don't have any money and nowhere to stay; how you really want to be done with me for good. Why would you say that shit and then be here in the room with me now and shit?

Like, what type of shit are you on?

The woman steps away from the man's face and holds out her hand.

WOMAN

Can I have my phone, please?

MAN

(Shaking his head, no stares at the woman and closes his eyes, begins yelling)

Fuck you and fuck your phone, for life! On my kids, I'm so done with you!

You are now dead to me.

The man violently smacks the phone towards the woman's hand. She swings her hand back, dodging the strike as the phone hits the floor. The woman slowly picks up her phone off the floor and stands up to face the man. She then slowly turns towards the door. With her back facing the man she speaks.

WOMAN

I'm sorry you had to read those texts. but… (pauses)…it's the truth.

I love you still.

The man turns towards the window. The woman opens the door and exits the hotel room.

END SCENE. FADES TO BLACK.

Waking up to him reading the messages I sent to my closest friends, I saw how hurt and betrayed he was. He was furious with me, and that was the narrative he committed to. We both were in that dark cheap-ass hotel room, upset with the truth. What he read was the truth. The fact that others knew was the truth. I had to be honest with myself about the manipulative spirit I was carrying which I often justified as my way of keeping the peace between us. We weren't being honest with ourselves or each other, and that was the absolute truth.

We finally separated for good. I was alone again, but this time I decided to change the channel from trauma to triumphant. I began taking an intensely deep look at myself in the mirror. Being alone allowed me to see that my ability to speak the truth had been on a series of back-to-back vacations. It was just lying on the beach of bad habits and bare minimums. It was finally time to wake up and open my eyes to all that I had created.

Acknowledgment of the truth held me back from saying many things in my life and almost held me back from writing this chapter and telling my story. I see exactly where and when I was not using my ability to speak the truth and accepting that it even existed. I see how good I became at quietly narrating a sick and sensational life of toxicity.

Today, I feel remarkably alive and enthusiastically alert. Most days, I'm in complete awe at how life speaks to me and how I've grown to respond responsibly. After two years, it turns out that the heart I was bleeding from was never broken, and the peace I was searching for was never missing. The truth is and will be that I was finally accepting my responsibility for everything I was experiencing. I decided to walk nobly with my obligations. The truth is what continues to set me free.

As my story finds you, may it offer you the empowerment to create regardless of your current situation or past decisions. No matter what, it is your responsibility to find a way to turn scraps into gold or create something out of nothing. The traces of your past do not define you; they only help you see that you are whole today. If you ever find yourself in need of uplifting, go and uplift another.

Action Steps

1: Trust your intuition. It is your fully-loaded weapon of mass creation. It will always guide you back into alignment.

2: Find a place of stillness and look into the mirror. Identify what is in you that you need to confront. Confront it, head on. Are you troubled by the past? Look into that and forgive yourself and anyone necessary for you to release that trouble and grow on.

3: Take full responsibility. A wise man said, "you deserve everything that has happened to you in life, but only the successful will admit it." Acknowledge what you've created, no matter how much you want to point the finger. Taking responsibility for your life gives you freedom no justice system or no Higher Power could ever grant.

Resources

www.noble-garb.com

IG pages

@noblegarb

@creator_flower

SIERRA M. CLARK
Reflections Of Her

Quote

"Every female child is genetically endowed with a unique code (path) to womanhood." - Feltis Thomas

Biography

International best selling author Sierra M. Clark was born in St. Petersburg Florida. She's the bloodline of her Belizean Grandfather. Sierra Clark is a Motivational Exhorter, Heart Coach, and Author. She has spent most of her life caring for others. Sierra loves what she does; she has over twenty years of experience in healthcare. She calls this hearting it forward. She's honored to say that she has been a CNA, HHA, and is currently a Patient Care Tech at her local Children's Hospital.

After writing her Bestselling author book "Finding Sierra".

Somehow, she knew it was time to heal using her words. She wanted to make a larger impact in the life of others, so Sierra has packaged her experiences, passion, and ability to hear hearts into her Exhortation Program, stimulating and transforming hearts.

Sierra Clark is also the founder of Transformation AcadeME which is the umbrella to her heart language and superpower.

That is joined together with the power of storytelling. Transformation AcadeMe is a Compilation, Exhortation, and Consulting Community. A Writing Enhancement and Life Enrichment Program. For individuals to discover the holistic benefits of writing.

Become the antidote, change their narrative and live beyond the story.

She inspires those she encounters to value themselves and live a better quality of life, inside out. She invites you and hopes you will join her on the path to discovering your unique antidote and methods that lead to daily clarity, self-fulfillment, and wealth.

Being a woman, what does that even mean? I don't think I put too much thought into being a woman. I knew I would grow up, become older, find a job, buy a house, get a car, and go to college. I now wondered, if even experiencing and having those things are signs of being a woman.

In the words of the owl in the Tootsie Pop commercial, "The world may never know". Honestly, until this moment I haven't had an intentional thought about what it takes to be a woman.

So, is it being a woman or do you become a woman? It was not until this very moment that I paused on the thought of what materials, if any, it took to be a woman. Really what does it mean to become a woman?

Who plays a part in a girl being or becoming a woman? What starts the journey into womanhood, and what are the telltale signs? Is there a way to truly know that a girl is now a woman?

Think about it for a moment, nature says a girl has entered a women's hood when she starts her menstrual cycle. Although not having this thought before now, with all respect to mother nature I think more is needed. I started my cycle later than some of my friends. Which would mean you could be a woman in middle or elementary school, due to mother nature knocking on the door.

I challenge all of these perspectives with my very own thought process as to what the meaning and qualifications of being or becoming a woman are. Is womanhood taught, like some would say manhood has to be? Or do you just learn it as you grow/experience life?

Let's assume that it is taught, and that is the mother who should do the teaching. Better yet let's SAY it is because you know the saying about when one assumes. And I'll have none of that in this chapter. I have done enough of that already if you ask me.

Now don't get me wrong there was enough of a lack to assist in the assumption, but I played my part in it also. If being a woman is to be taught, let's start with my earliest memories of my mother. Please follow along, it truly gets interesting. Let's thicken the plot, why don't we?

Here's the backdrop, let me take you to a time, I remember a time when in school others would be teased due to not having a two-parent household. There was a stigma that if you didn't have that, then you lacked something. Let's stay here for a moment, allow me to paint the picture for you. I had a mom and dad who worked 9 to 5. A sister I would remember mom would dress us like that, and I had an older brother. So, I had the ideal life according to society and the kids who bullied other kids if they didn't.

On one summer afternoon, my world came crashing down, to a 9-year-old that's what it felt like. I titled this Identity crisis in my first book, allowing me to keep painting this picture. I remember my grandmother would often call me and my little cousins in her room one by one and give us a sweet treat. It was always a delight for us. I called it my yum yum time. I was either sitting on the side of her bed or in the chair that sat in the corner. It was still fuzzy. My sounds of yum yum were hit with mass destruction. When her words meet my eardrums, they echoed Patti is not your mother.

I'm still unsure how, to sum up, these feelings. Just like that, I went from having the ideal household to utter confusion. Time stood still, and things were never the same. This shattered my desire to be a daddy's girl. So, the dad I had known was just erased from my story and never replaced with another father. My sister and brother turn out to be my first cousins. Mom was my auntie, she was my biological mother's younger sister. I'm not sure if my grandmother made the announcement, but everything and everyone felt different.

Let me ask the question again, who teaches a girl to become a woman? Is it just the responsibility of the woman who births her? If so, then my new normal didn't offer the best ingredients to ensure I would.

My biological mom came with conditions some might say definitely stop her from even being able to play a part in me being or becoming a woman. My sister and brother's cousins had no problem cracking their crackhead jokes. I never remember anyone stopping them. Yep, her condition was a drug problem.

My household no longer felt like home. This altered a lot. I didn't have the typical mother or the typical childhood experience of falling in love with a woman who gave birth to me. Because she taught me about the birds and the bees, because she took me to the store to buy my first tampons, or she was the one picking me up from school and helping me get dressed for prom.

They called her Duke, and all I knew about her at this point was that she was addicted to cocaine, not because I saw her that way; I think I was the only one able to see past it. But solely due to this was all being said about her, about this woman. I now ask who played the role for her and who taught her about being and becoming a woman. I can't say whether I even remember seeing my birth mother before this point or not. Due to other family members openly talking about it, there was no escaping the fact that my biological mother came with a condition.

Would this or could this condition stop her from the part she played in me becoming a woman? Was she automatically disqualified because of it???

As time would have it, I grew to understand that even with this condition, she was my biological mother. And no matter the conditions, ain't a woman alive that can take my momma's place **(In my 2Pac voice)**

My definition of what makes a girl become a woman is her intentional ability to see past another woman's condition and respect her for her position. This was my permission then to know that I had every right to see my reflection in the woman who gave me life despite her human condition.

This is my chapter, so here is my opinion, whoever can see their reflection in another woman has passed my requirements of what it means to be a woman. Another thing I learned was that we all have human conditions.

Don't miss the opportunity to admire a woman. Now I'll admit as growing up, I had great examples of women in my life. This concept could be missed or overlooked if you're looking at a woman from her life condition, not the position she holds in life.

I didn't know much about this woman I now called mother. Everyone would proudly say, no one would let me forget, that she (had a condition) was a crackhead. And the story around crackheads was always bad, always explained as if they were just some types of evil, not good, nor worthy of respect. To a (little girl) person who didn't know at the time that she had the gift to see past all of that. To a (little girl) person who just wanted to know more about her.

I remember being worried that I would get in trouble if I told those who spoke this way of her; I could see something different.

My heart just wouldn't let me, only be ok with this picture being painted of her. My heart smiles at this very moment for two reasons. Writing this just helped me experience in real-time the holistic benefits of writing. As I sat here typing that, this polished the smile in my heart when I wrote this. 2. It makes me feel good about myself and the woman I've become.

I realized we all have the power of choice, and I value who I've become as a woman. The beauty of my characteristic is when I'm shown the reflection of who I am in another woman's (reflection) condition and position. I discovered, well more so, stumbled upon the essence of being a woman. There is a big difference between essence and sexuality.

Learning that, once I could see my essence, I'm now able to see it in all women, no matter their shape, color, and size of another woman. This was the beginning of my being able to see even deeper through the conditions of a woman.

Expanding my ability to see that in their conditions, they are flowers. The ability to see you not as a seed but the beautiful flower inside, most times before the individual could.

I later joined the Miss Fashion Global Modeling Competition. To intentionally allow me to be in the garden of other flowers. I was going to walk the runway with 499 other women.

Due to some of the things that society has projected, I almost got caught up on not feeling good enough, skinny enough, and lacking the things a model needed to be a model. This felt like the same feeling I felt when I assumed that because my mom was addicted to cocaine, it meant I lacked something; I needed to be a woman.

Is being a woman about whether you can give birth or how much pain you can take? I can see that there is so much more than what we assume is obvious in being/becoming a woman.

To be in the room with 499 different women scared me, but I did it anyway. This brought me so much joy at the same time.

What will make me stand out in a room full of other women who are perhaps more beautiful than me, who make more money than me, and who have more experience than me? All of this could be correct and more. But I, too, now can see past my donations, revealing being uniquely me was the only thing that could make me stand out. It had to be my confidence, my assuredness, and my understanding that I am a rose and mesmerizing all by myself.

If I'm a rose, you can pick what flower you see yourself as. This can be a pretty reminder to see a woman regardless of their positions in our lives as dandelions, tulips, daffodils, lotus, and sunflowers. And when you join us together, women become the bouquet of life.

Change your perspective and allow yourself the privilege to see that God fearfully and wonderfully created all of us to be one-of-a-kind masterpieces. The fact is that we're created in all shapes, colors, and sizes and are the very things that make us uniquely beautiful.

I now see my reflection in every woman I meet. The ones I come directly in contact with, the ones I see across the way pushing a stroller, and the ones walking on the side of the road, holding a sign that reads hungry and needs money for food.

When you envy another woman or even feel the competition, it means you're only focused on that woman's (condition) outward appearance, not her (position) beauty within.

*I'm proud to say that my mom has been drug and alcohol-free for over 13 years. See, I knew I saw more; I just knew it was more to her than just her condition. Just like it's more to you. Do me a favor, don't just stop to smell the (**roses**) flowers, but see yourself as one.*

R. reflections

O. of

S. self

E. empowerment

-SMC

Action Steps

1. Disrupt- Outdated words, thoughts, and toxic behaviors. Removing all the M.U.S made-up stuff you believed or placed on yourself. It is perfectly ok to redefine yourself so your feelings and habits reflect the life you desire. One way to do this is to write your name on a piece of paper and for each letter in your name write an adjective, then define the meaning of that word.

Be intentional with each letter in your name, (write) speak those things that are not as though they were. Then put it in a place where you can see it, so it can be your constant reminder of the new and intentional you.

2. Transform- Your perspective of self will open you up to seeing the beauty in yourself, then others. Handling yourself with grace, knowing that there are no such things as mistakes, just lessons. What you titled as a mistake, disappointment, and uncertainty are all part of the human experience.

Allow yourself to focus on seeing the result you want to have with them and love them beyond their conditions. Happily releasing old stories, letting go of who did or didn't do what, the should of and could of and would of's.

3. *Tame- Yourself to have an open perspective. This will help you see your parents from their human position, not their human condition. Remove the expectation you have for them and the obligations of that person being your parent or whatever relationship status you have with them. This will help you to see (your parent) that this individual is a human with feelings, and regrets also. They have emotions too. Doing that is a constant reminder that those you love are human. This collapses time allowing you to live in the moment. Plan out a regular day and time, to be intentional and talk to them. Find out their favorite salad dressing, what their hopes and dreams are, their favorite middle school teacher, etc. Seeing them as a stranger will allow you to learn things about them you never knew.*

Resources

SierraClark.life

Info@Sierra Clark.life

IG smcwarrior

KENYA A. HOOVER
Removing The Labels

Quote

"Without work, the magic won't come." -Jay Z

Biography

Kenya is a mother, Motivational Keynote Speaker, Poet, Podcast Creator, Executive Career Coach, Certified Lean Six Sigma Green Belt and Lean Practitioner. Kenya is the CEO & Co-Founder of We Power Executives, LLC., providing top-notch executive services to Small to Medium Businesses. Kenya and her team are "Redefining Executives of tomorrow".

For most of my career I was told that I am too aggressive, too masculine, and too urban. I have been perceived as having too high of morals and that I care too much about the people and not the objectives. One of my former bosses said to me during a performance review that my thought process was unusual, and different and it would make it challenging for anyone to follow me as a leader. I recall during an interview early in my career, the hiring manager told me that since I knew more than him, I was not coachable...we all know how that turned out, no job offers for me.

My career spans over 22 years and for the first 15 years of my career, I believed that I was not good enough, or strong enough to be a leader. I began to wear the labels that others had placed on me. So, I started to minimize myself and "fit" into the suite of others. I wanted to be a leader, so I followed and mimicked those who didn't look like me or act like me but were in the roles I wanted to be in. I put on a suit that did not fit me.

The most pivotal point in my career was when I was part of a layoff. This was not your standard layoff to reduce cost; no, it was to reduce people who the General Manager did not like; it was personal. I had worked so hard. I joined the team as an individual contributor and exceeded the sales goals. I was promoted twice, leading a Sales Enablement/onboarding team and an Inside Sales Team, and in both roles, I built a high-performing team that crushed every goal and every obstacle. During that time, I started to find my voice as a leader. I started to remove the labels and stopped doubting myself.

About 75 days prior to my being laid off, I was in a dark place. I wanted to give up because my boss had moved onto a new team within the company; our General Manager was a bully and made it clear that he did not care for me. He did not want me to be promoted and tried to do everything to make me fail. The irony is that I didn't fail, I actually got better and stronger. Well, at the time I didn't know how strong I really was. I would come into work and fight back my tears. I questioned my actions, my strategies, and even my intelligence. In order for me to keep calm and not break down in front of my sales team; I would play John Coltrane's song Kulu Se Mama and Carla Harris' speech from the 2016 MA Conference for Women.

For those 75 days prior to my being laid off, the first 30 minutes of my day was me pushing through the uneasy feeling and that negative energy that consumed me as soon as I walked into the building. It was like I couldn't breathe or move; I was lost. I had started working on an exit plan before the layoff because I knew that if I stayed, I would not survive mentally nor physically. I realized that I had to "live" for my daughter and mother. So, when I was called into the office with HR, I knew that I was going to be fired. This stillness came over me, and I wasn't afraid. I went through the process, but in the end, I came out on top.

The HR person, who looked like me, told me that she had never had anyone remain so professional and poised during the process. I looked at her and told her that she was just doing her job and that I had no ill feelings toward her. She stopped the process and told me that she was going to help me find a new role within the company. She said it would be in the company's best interest to retain top talent. All the doubt I had of myself, just went away at that moment. I was being seen, understood, and recognized, not labeled.

Within a week, I had a new role within the company and I was back with my former boss, who had left for a new role. I thought, yes, now I can be "free". For the next 6 years, I would experience the same labeling. I had a new fight on my hands but this time, I was prepared. I did not compromise myself, my team, not my morals. I stayed the course and designed a process and built an elite, high-performing global team. I would sit at tables and call out anyone who dismissed, disrespected, displaced, or even disenfranchised me or my team. I would slide those "black labels" right back to anyone who tried to put them on me.

This was my test. I told myself that I would not be Sisyphus. I wasn't going to sell my soul to the labels of others, wear a suit that did not fit me, or become minimized. I would remain true to myself. I was able to drive results, and do things that I was told in the past that I could not do. I was leading a team that was in 4 regions and making an impact by building a career legacy.

As I was growing and achieving my goals, I set a new mission for myself. I wanted to be a Director by the time I was 45. I started to work towards that goal, I hit every box on the "Director checklist". It became clear that I was boxed in, that I would not be a Director; well, not at that company. I knew it was time to move on when I asked for more responsibility and my VP at the time told me that if I did that, who would do what I do? I was more valuable in my current role. I did that laugh you do when someone doubts you, yeah that laugh.

He was right, I was valuable in that role. When I accepted a Director position at another company, it was clear that what I had done would fall apart. I became a Director sixteen days before my forty-fifth birthday! I had achieved my goal. I went for it and didn't look back. I no longer doubt my worth, my abilities, my thought processes, my voice, and my intelligence. I don't allow others to label me or define me.

In my Director role, it became clear that I am too much for the space I am in. Carla Harris said it best in her 2016 MA Conference for Women speech," Pearl #4: If you have a guy or a gal that thinks you are too much for them, they are right. Never ever apologize for your accomplishments. Never apologize for your hard work and where it has gotten you. Never cover your light for somebody else's convenience. Own all of who you are; if that person thinks that you are too much, there is one word 'Next ".

I am now on my "Next" journey. I am the CEO and Co-Found of We Power Executives. We are redefining Executives for tomorrow. We are removing the labels of who and what an Executive looks like. Our mission is to coach top talent and match them not only with the right position but the right company. We strive to be efficient, authentic, diverse, and inclusive in our approach, which empowers our clients to be successful."

We work for both the individual candidate and the business to align core values, strengths, talent, and growth opportunities. My goal is to influence the next chapter of Executives on a global scale. If I remained in my corporate space, I would continue to be overlooked, minimized, dismissed, displaced, disrespected, and just "dissed". I accept that I am bigger than the box I was placed in. My ancestors and parents fought too hard for me not to shine!

I don't know who said this quote, but is part of my personal philosophy, "Real success is success with self; it's not having things, but in having mastery, having victory over oneself"

I have learned so many things through my career journey. There are a few lessons that have carried me through. One is that I define myself. My mother always told me that I would be behind the eight ball twice; because I am a female and black. I wasn't always comfortable with my name or my outward appearance. I wanted to" modify" myself to fit others.

As I got older, I realized that I could remove these ideas that black women weren't strong, beautiful, or smart enough to be leaders. I celebrate my victories and those who look like me, I celebrate with them too. The perception that others have of me before they meet me, is a welcoming opportunity for me to reintroduce myself.

I don't get mad or upset, because that's their perception and it's my responsibility to coach them. I no longer look at the "black labels" as my labels; I kindly return them and show them who I am, who Kenya is. Own your narrative, be your storyteller, and don't live in others' fantasies of who you are.

I also have learned that it's okay to cry and release the pain, the energy that is holding you back. When I was laid off and walked out of the building I got in my car and cried and banged on the steering wheel.

I had a Florida Evans moment from "Good Times" when James died and she screamed "Damn, Damn, Damn" and dropped the glass bowl; I had that moment. It was a painful moment but freeing at the same time. In most black communities, we are taught not to cry; it is a sign of weakness. Black women are often perceived as being weak, so if we cry, we are showing signs of weakness. That is so not true. These myths aren't even ours; we have been conditioned to believe things about ourselves that aren't even of ourselves. So, sis, I say cry and scream and drop that glass bowl?

Another life-changing lesson I have learned is that I am a warrior. I have overcome so many obstacles and push through some rough terrain. Don't doubt your strength. We have and will have moments when we want to give up.

I remember being in an executive meeting and providing a solution for the issue, and the executives dismissed me in such an unintentional intentional way. In the next breath, someone who doesn't look like me said the same thing and everyone listened and gave praise.

I wanted to get up and exit the room, well, leave the call; I couldn't have the dramatic effect. Instead, I kept my emotional intelligence intact and called them all out and said how interesting it was that when this other person said the same thing it was validated but when I said it first, it was dismissed. The silence was so loud, that no matter what came next, it was clear that I was not going to be silenced. James Fortune's song "Live Through It" is part of my life's playlist. In the middle of the song, the lyrics speak volumes:

I know you're saying now

There's no way I can live through this.

But Live through it

No one can understand all that you have been dealing with

You're dying inside (dying inside)

You're in the fight of your life

But God knows (but God Knows)

And He's there (and He's there)

And you will

Live through it

Grow through it

Get through it

You can Live through it

You can Live through it

It's working for your good.

Finally, I have learned forgiveness. I have learned to be comfortable with being me. During my journey, I have discovered my pain, my triggers, and my victories. As I started to remove the labels, I had moments when I would ask myself, "What were you thinking". I had to become vulnerable enough with myself to say, "I did the best I could at that moment, and I am sorry". I had to become honest in my pain and say to myself, "Forgive me for...", and I started to list all the things and situations I needed to forgive myself for. This was not easy or the most comfortable moment, but my healing began and I became stronger. Put in the work for you and your magic will come.

Suite up and armor up and fight for yourself. You are strong and mighty. You will overcome this challenge and come out triumphant. Keep in mind that what happens next may not be on your time but on a much higher power's time.

Action Steps

I am often asked what I do to stay focused, calm and balanced. There are several things I do throughout my day and journey but the following three things are consistent and part of my daily, weekly and monthly routine.

1. Journaling

I know some of you may not like to write or may say "I don't have the time". Invest in a notebook or a journal; you can use your phone's notes or voice recorder. This is how you make a self-commitment. Take the time each day to reflect by journaling. This will allow you a safe space to express yourself and release your pain; have your Florida Evans moment or celebrate your victories. Journaling is a judgmental free space.

2. Me Time

Take time for yourself every day. Our lives can become so consumed by work, family, and various things that we forget ourselves. Find moments throughout the day where you can have "me time". For instance, when you grab a cup of coffee or tea, enjoy that cup alone in a quiet place. Take a 5-minute walk alone or take yourself on a date. Play your favorite song and dance in the middle of the room. Taking daily "me time" will become freeing and rewarding. This time will allow you to get to know who you have become, how strong you are, and how you are worthy of happiness and greatness.

3. Form a Community/Village

I formed a tight community of two close friends who kept me grounded through my personal and professional challenges. We formed a village, we are each other's truth, cheerleaders, coaches, and motivation. When I was doubting myself, these two stepped in and balanced me. They kept me pushing through. If you don't have that community/village, I recommend finding a Career or Executive Coach.

Resources

To Find Out More About Kenya visit

Email: Kenya@wepowerexecutives.com

www.wepowerexecutive.com

CHANTAL PEREIRA
Finding Your Frequency

Quote

"May your focus be sharp, faith be strong, and the power of your frequency be felt by everyone blessed by your presence."

Biography

Chantal Pereira is a wife, mother of three teens, and believer. As an Executive in the Strategic and Operational planning field, she has been a leader in numerous industries over the last 20 years, including telecommunications, medical device, and nonprofit and federal contracting, to help organizations to operate with excellence. Chantal has also dedicated her career to serving youth, and families, as well as minority small businesses and nonprofits. Chantal considers herself a "momvestor", as she consciously dedicates her focus to cultivating a home where creativity, discovery, and entrepreneurship are explored with her children. She also advocates and teaches self-care principles with the mission of helping others find their frequency. Walking out the journey with others of returning home to a life of clarity of who you are, who you are and one's purpose is her mission. Her unique approach to learning to align one's energy through self-discovery along with the intention of bringing harmony to all areas of life is one of her greatest and most fulfilling joys.

When I think ack to 2004, I was at what I believed to be the peak of happiness. I had had my first son and was going to be blessed with my first daughter. Being a mother had brought me such immeasurable joy, and I had my mother to thank for that. She was a single parent with a large family as support and so love overflowed, laughter and attention were rich and the feeling of being supported was consistent for me. Her presence, guidance, wisdom, and warmth were woven into so many experiences with her and my family that it made me want that for myself.

And so, with the blessing of my daughter Ozara, came a new chapter of learning to raise a Queen just as my mother had. What I hadn't anticipated was that it was also the final chapter of life for my mother who was the one person who breathed life into my hardest times and cheered me on throughout all circumstances. My mother was diagnosed with stage 4 multiple myeloma and passed at the early age of 66, five months after my first princess's birth.

I quickly became a caregiver at a time when I thought I needed her most, and in turn, she needed me to be there the way she had been for 26 years of my life. I was devastated, lost, and scared all while putting on the bravest face, I knew possible.

I knew the inevitable was near and did the best that I could. To this day I remember running errands, and my aunt calling me from the hospice to say "Chantal, she's holding on. I think she's waiting on you". I asked to speak to her and said "Mommy, I love you. You've done all you can and if this is too much, know that it was always more than enough". I was told that 11 minutes later she had passed, and my best friend was gone. In one week, I had planned a funeral and all that comes with a loved one's death all while my emotions and mind were in overload from talking to so many people yet feeling so alone.

Ephesians 3:20: Now all glory to God, who is able, through his mighty power at work within us, to accomplish infinitely more than we might ask or think.

From the outside, I showed up as this strong, organized, and together daughter; inside, I felt hollow. Yearning for one last time to hear her call me "Buttercup," for one last breakfast with her, one last moment to listen to her favorite music, one last chance to be in her presence. One last thing.

Week after week, it seemed like everything went back to normal for everyone around me, and I was stuck in grief and a gut-

wrenching feeling of lack. Looking at her pictures and recalling a flood of memories looped in my mind. I would remind myself that it takes time to get through the stages of grief when all I was focused on was wanting more time with her.

Until that point, I had all these love experiences but not many losses like this. This unknowingly became the beginning of a new journey to what I see as the self-care lifestyle. It started in my silence. Waking up in the morning, choosing to be still and just be. That stillness brought a floodgate of power and peace. It was as if God said 'Chantal... Your mother was a full reflection of love, you are too.

What will you choose today?". As silly as it sounds, as soon as the notion that I had a choice to see this as a way to continue her demonstration of love from her through me, I realized the higher calling in all of this. Starting my day doing small things to align myself and my energy before seeing anyone else in the house was my responsibility. Seeing my children and feeling her love in them couldn't be ignored. I remember months later hearing one of her favorite songs, seeing her favorite perfume bottle in a store, and so many other little nudges whether by divine intervention, my own manifestation, or sheer coincidence that I saw a gentle nudge that all was well.

I began giving more time to cultivating moments and experiences and being intentional about making my surroundings feel like home with my inner being and everyone around me. The possibility of taking time for granted wasn't received in fear

but as a desire to make the most of it no matter the circumstance. Filtering by day, sharpening my focus, and facing the middle point where my fear and faith battled was enlightening. At that point, I accepted that even faith, true faith wasn't just an idea; it is a conscious acceptance of having no control while showing up to the calling on my life that I was required to act on.

It took me years to realize that what I lost physically would always remain in my being and spirit. The essence of grief when we learn to nurture and tend to our inner being with love becomes a catalyst in finding our true self... in fact-finding our frequency. It is our unique vibration, flow, and energy that serves us to show up as our best self while our overflow blesses others. We can dedicate each day to surrendering to the notion that living a life well lived includes a conscious dedication to loving ourselves and others despite any circumstance and learning that an overflowing cup doesn't happen by itself.

Self-care isn't one thing. It's a rich recipe of all things that nourish our soul, bring peace, clarity, consciousness, and connection to ourselves and others as we navigate life. It changes with every season, and it's our duty to remain conscious of our needs and to tend to them as diligently as we tend to other things so we can show up to life in wholeness. There is something about seeing your soul as home, seeing the evolution and growth of love within you overflow despite what your eyes may see and your mind may think. Our ability to align with our strength while remaining vulnerable to life's ripples makes space for your blessings. Exceeding and Abundant blessings. Blessings that we will never be able to measure but bring overwhelming joy to our souls.

When you have to face yourself, and all that dwells from within during difficult times without the things and people you thought made us stronger, you learn the strength was always there. They were just a beautiful reflection of the magnificence they saw in you. Doesn't that become a reason to continue pursuing your greatness? I'm not saying to not grieve; I'm calling us to walk out that journey until you see, feel and accept that greater calling.

I pray every reader that comes across this book surrenders to the deserved journey of self-care. Aligning from within will attract a tribe that will help you along the way so that loss doesn't feel that way. This is a legacy calling.... A calling to dig deep, sow new seeds and cultivate a life well lived. It will strip you of the identity you've hidden behind and pour in all the needed love, support, light, and laughter your soul desires. You'll relearn the true essence of love in action from people and experiences you would never have explored if it weren't for the moments, we experience loss.

I write this as an example of standing in the gap for those who need the reminder that light and good energy exist in all things. No, everything isn't perfect, but there is another reality amidst the reality we have taught ourselves to acknowledge, and there is no greater time than now to receive, align, and pursue a life well lived.

These realizations sprouted as I became more inclined to focus on solutions and my connections with relationships that matter. I was still feeling the loss but understood that the only way to keep my power and peace was to walk, stay present, give myself the grace to process my thoughts, feelings, and emotions in truth, and then move forward. Some days it was one step, others were a mile, but my duty to me was to move forward.

A conscious regard for the importance of having a healthy mind, body, and soul is essential to the understanding that with any kind of grief, you must also allow grace and gratitude to collide. We will come across people who deal with loss in so many different ways and with some who have never experienced it. As I watch my children blossom, I consider these things:

- What can I do to show love and honor the legacy set before me?

- What can I do to shield them from some of the ways of the world, but not shelter them from the world and what the loss may look like.

- *How can I teach through my example that you can experience loss and emerge from it with a greater sense of self and of others.*

Our frequency is a gift. What does our presence present to ourselves and those who matter most to us? We don't always have to agree with all the things life serves us, but if we can align to the notion that life is still here to serve us, we will navigate life with greater joy and fulfillment. What I labeled as a void from the loss of my mother, I fill with new experiences and opportunities to share with my children the greatest desire to see them flourish with love, in love, and in alignment that I am just a reflection of all the goodness within themselves. Laugh often, live courageously, and love immensely, starting with you first.

Action steps

1. Pick your Peace

We have a choice every single day to choose peace of mind and joy from within despite any outside circumstance. From the minute we put our feet on the ground in the morning until we close our eyes at night- think about how you use your energy and where you put it. It's okay to realign so you take the time you need to be in a whole space. Make your home your sanctuary, surround yourself with those who elevate your mind and spirit, and decide to make this life about your existence and legacy.

2. Cultivate a Life Well Lived

Define what a life well lived means to you. The significance and value you place upon that should be the starting place to dedicate time and effort in that pursuit. To cultivate is an action, a daily practice of focusing on doing the things that are meaningful and being open to receiving all that aligns with you. When you think of the memories left within others and things you would love to do... follow those things and cherish and share those moments.

3. Have beautiful conversations with yourself and those that bring harmony to your soul.

Speak. Share your thoughts, feelings, growth, grief, and desires with an inner circle that feels like home. Eventually, what had you stuck within will come up and out, received with support, love, and reflection to receive what can help your heart mend and bring peace to your soul. Our experiences, transparency, and vulnerability are possible lifelines for someone else, even though our loss.

Resources

Website:www.findingyourfrequency.com

1 Social Media Handle: IG Chan_Pereira,

IG Jaoke_LLC

CONCLUSION

Superlative Woman is a riveting tale about how Superlative women stood up to their WHY. They took the courageous step of shining light in dark places. Their experiences prove to be ultra-transformational and life-changing. They leave you with action steps that are life-changing and sure to help you heal holistically from the inside out.

The action steps teach you how a life of mishaps, obstacles, and setbacks can become a launching pad to a fuller, more extraordinary life, and future.

They demonstrate what happens when one pauses, reflects, and takes on life's dark shadows. A revelation revealed how walking through the shadows of life proved to be a blessing in disguise.

A disguise that revealed a remarkable strength, and amazing inner healing you never thought possible that lay within by standing up.

Stand Up.

Stand UP to your story, Be your own hero.

1. **Vision-** *Highlighting Women's unspoken strength, that allowed them to find strength in the dark.*

2. **Mission-** *To help 1,000 women yearly give their experience a voice, connect, and see the beauty in another woman.*

3. **Values-** *Self-awareness, Diversity, Community, Holistically, and Service*

4. **Purpose-** *To inspire people to be the light in every chapter of life, allowing them to heal on purpose.*

Uses Of Foundations

1. The main use of foundation is structural stability. ...
2. Furthermore, the foundation is used to distribute the weight. ...
3. Without a foundation, a building would simply sink during natural calamities. ...
4. For the construction of a building, the surface needs to be at the same level. ...
5. Every location or area doesn't have the same type of soil. ...
6. Foundation increases the durability of the building. ...

ABOUT THE VISIONARY AUTHORS

Wanda Hawkins is a Family Nurse Practitioner (FNPc). She was born in Chicago, Illinois, is the 5th child of nine siblings, and is also a widow whose partner supported her throughout her career. She attended Chamberlain College of Nursing and earned a Master of Science Degree in Nursing MSN (FNP) with a specialty in (Psychiatry). She is also a member of the honorary nurse's society Sigma Theta Tau. She spent most of her adult years in Atlanta, Georgia, where she worked as a registered nurse (RN) at the Trauma Care Center of Grady Health Care System in cardiology nurse care. She later branched into the specialty of psychiatric care. Specialty care netted her Travel Nurse Contractual assignments with John Hopkins hospital in Baltimore, Maryland, George Washington hospital in Washington, DC., and many other projects throughout the United States.

She later attended True Way Seminary College, receiving a Master's Degree in Divinity (M.Div.). She is an ordained minister and a peacetime United States veteran. She is co-founder of Focus on Family Faith and Action (Foffia), a one-stop shop shelter facility for homeless women, children, and women who struggle with addictions. She has a passion for working with young women. She spearheads a mentorship model that provides one-

on-one instruction on a build-back better pathway on becoming your best self with a relatively easy step-to-step model.

Today she has walked into new frontiers and found a passion for writing. She is the founder of UltimatePrimeAuthor.com, a platform to introduce new authors to the holistic approach of healing from the inside out through their writing. She also is an author, empowerment coach, speaker, and health and wellness practitioner. Her first of three books were pre-launched last year. (Poverty to Prosperity) is about how a simple mindset transition can transform one's defeats into that of abundance.

Sierra Clark was born to a Honduran grandfather. She's a beloved daughter, friend, servant, and light unto the world. She is brave, strong, fun, loving, and intuitive. Sierra is a community builder and takes great pride in being a part of the village that helps to raise adults and children. Sierra Clark is a motivational speaker, exhorter heart coach, and author. She has spent most of her life caring for others.

Sierra loves what she does. She is spontaneous and trusting; she has over 20 years of experience in healthcare and she's a best-selling author of the book, Finding Sierra. Somehow, she knew it was time to heal with her words.

She wanted to make a more significant impact in the lives of others, so she packed her experiences and passions and her ability to hear the hearts into her Compilation Exhortation Program. Enhancing and enriching the hearts of others.

Sierra is spiritually aware that she brings light to this planet. She has always been enthusiastic about others' growth and success. She loves when others are awakened to the beauty in themselves. Sierra Clark is also the founder of Transformation AcadeMe which uses the power of storytelling and art to disrupt outdated communication tame limited belief and transform individuals from the inside out.

THE CO-FOUNDERS AND AUTHORS